The Whole Truth
& NOTHING BUT THE TRUTH,
So Help Me Teachers!

Hear the battlecry of eleven educators sharing their unadulterated truths in and outside the classroom

Copyright © 2017 Vicki Kirk May. All Rights Reserved. Published by Jai the Author Publishing. No part of this book may be reproduced, distributed or transmitted in any form by any means, graphics, electronics, mechanical, photocopying, recording, or any other without written permission from the publisher.

Book Cover illustrated by Mr. Eric Kirk

Printed in the United States of America

ISBN-13: 978-0692047651

ISBN-10: 0692047654

The Whole Truth & Nothing But the Truth, So Help Me Teachers!

Table of Contents

Dedication 1

Message from the Compiler 2

Foreword 4

PART ONE: The Curriculum Revealed 5

Vicki Kirk May 6
    Rise & Shine, But Rise Even if You Don't Shine   6

Dr. Ragan Brown 19
    I'm Done, I Quit, It's Over   19

Dr. Marquita Blades 28
    The Mediocre Teacher   28

Nicole Brown-Horston 36
    In Loving Memory of Grandma   36

Tamika L. Blythers 40
    I Made A Vow   40

Andrea Gibbs 49
    Will I Ever Pass This Test?   49

PART TWO: Lessons Learned 59

Vicki Kirk May 60
    They Are Out To Kill Me!   60

Dr. Marquita Blades 69
    It's Okay To Teach Who You Love   69

Nicole Brown-Horston 77
    I Am Somebody   77

Andrea Gibbs 81
    Will I Ever Get a Job?   81

The Whole Truth & Nothing But the Truth, So Help Me Teachers!

PART THREE: Class in Session..............................**89**

Teresa Thomas 90
    Wake Up America!   90

Dalila Spratt..97
    The Good, Bad & Ugly   97

Katherine Lyons Bester 104
    Lessons Along the Way   104

Carole Cramer-Banks 118
    A Moment of Transparency   118

Delores "Magnolia" Walker..123
    A Simple Reminder   123

Acknowledgments 127

About the Compiler..128

The Whole Truth & Nothing But the Truth, So Help Me Teachers!

Dedication

To my beautiful loving mother who gave me the choice to work or attend college and pursue my purpose. You giving me the freedom to choose changed my life.

— Vicki Kirk May

The Whole Truth & Nothing But the Truth, So Help Me Teachers!

Message from the Compiler

VICKI KIRK MAY

"Honesty is the first chapter in the book of wisdom."
- Thomas Jefferson

I have heard so many sayings about the truth from 'the truth hurts' to 'why lie when the truth will do'. As I began this writing project, I began considering my truth. I mean, my real truth. Not the truth I wanted everyone to see, but the truth that I wanted to keep hidden where no one could gain entrance but GOD and me. We all hold deep dark secrets that we want to take to the grave. Those truths that you cannot imagine saying out loud because of the judgement that comes with the revelation.

In this book, you will hear the heart of educators who explored their truth and experienced the awakening of freedom along the way. Choosing to tell your truth knowing that it may not be perceived as true by others can be difficult, but most of all a lonely place. It is at the place called isolation that these authors were able to pour out their truth and release to whomever is willing to stand under the flow and receive.

Silence can sometimes be deafening but no longer will the screams of silence be heard louder than the resounding voice of Truth. Whether your truth is being overwhelmed with paper; emotional and social trumping the academic concerns of students; living paycheck to paycheck; over-worked and under-appreciated; impacting the lives of children; or the total enjoyment of teaching, it is your truth... so own it! As you read this book, allow yourself to find and experience your truth in the revelation of others' truth.

I pray that this book is the answer to your questions, the solution to your problems, the light to your dark place, and the hope to your discouragement.

From this day forth let the truth reverberate in our homes, schools, churches, businesses, and the world so immensely forcing the inevitable change to greatness we all desire.

And the truth shall make you free!

The Whole Truth & Nothing But the Truth, So Help Me Teachers!

Foreword

By Pastor Michael D. McClure, Sr.
Revelation Church in Irondale, Alabama

By definition, Truth is a fact or belief that is accepted as true. Truth is most often used to mean being in accord with fact or standard. Ever so valuable, Truth is a commodity that's quickly becoming a rarity.

If Truth is to be preserved and honored, then it must be told as often and as strong as possible. Therefore those bearing the Truth are encouraged throughout the pages of this book to be dedicated and courageous to not ever allow the Truth to fade, flounder, fail or falter.

If the world in which we all live, love, learn, lead and laugh in is to continue to exist, and life as we know it continues to prevail and prosper, then Truth must be the cornerstone of all reality.

So in closing I submit this to all: tell the Truth, be ready and willing at all times! Let the Truth be what girds, guides and grounds you, and the Truth will set you free.

The Whole Truth & Nothing But the Truth, So Help Me Teachers!

PART ONE: THE CURRICULUM REVEALED

The Whole Truth & Nothing But the Truth, So Help Me Teachers!

Rise & Shine, But Rise Even if You Don't Shine

Maxine Johnson, married at age 17 and soon after, while still being a child herself, was responsible for four lives. Yep, Maxine was a proud mother of four children!

I think we were poor in theory, and I laugh as I write this because we never felt poor. Somehow Mama (Maxine) always made sure we had the best that she could afford.

"Take your clothes off when you come home from school!" "Don't run in and out this house!" "Cut the lights off!" "Shut the door letting out my air!" I really could go on and on. Oh, wait a minute, one more, "I'm gonna whoop you for old and new!" We all cringed when we heard that one!

I'm laughing on the inside just thinking about how scared we were at the thought of what that meant. However, at this moment in my life the one thing that I remember her saying that has literally changed my life and the way I show up in the world is, "Rise and shine, rise even if you don't shine!"

As a child, those words aggravated and annoyed me to no end. Those words interrupted my sleep. Those words meant it was time to do what I didn't want to do. They were a constant reminder that my mom had a cruel sense of humor. Little did I know it would be those very same words that would now become one of my mantras. All of her children, all four of us, now say it to our children. Those words would become engraved into our lifestyle to keep us going. "Rise, even if you don't shine."

The truth and nothing but the truth sounds pretty simple, right? My head is spinning wondering where to begin, what to say, what not to say. Finally a still, soft, authoritative, kind voice said, "Tell your truth, for the truth shall make you free."

My truth is a real-time truth. It is not just in my past, but it is happening right now as I write. My truth is: there are days when I wonder if I am necessary. I wonder if I am the voice to whom my mentees should listen, the shoulder my friends should cry, the mother, wife, teacher, entrepreneur, minister, or Elder. The whole truth and nothing but the truth, there will be days you do not want to teach. If anyone tells you they want to teach every day, something is fishy in Denmark, as the old saying goes.

I love teaching but there are some days I just don't want to teach. Some may say, 'Then how can that be your passion?' 'How can you say you have been called to teach?' My answer is easy.

My story may not even be a story, but rather a guide to rising up even when everything inside you says to STAY DOWN! I had been at the same school for over 15 years. My school was a second home and my co-workers were my extended family. However, something happened. I can't pinpoint when but I do know that one day I walked into my classroom and it felt like I was suffocating. I could not breathe.

The entire day I taught but all the while thinking about being at home, the store, church, anywhere but in that classroom. Regardless of how I felt, I went back the next day, and the next day, and the next day until finally I no longer thought of all the places I could go. I settled for being where I was... in my classroom.

The dreamer had no more dreams. Life had slowly killed my dreams and, sadly, I did not even know it. I called it focusing on my career, or being sensible, or not being stupid, or, my favorite, being grateful to have a job.

Truth be told, no one killed my dreams but me. I committed passion suicide. The very thing I loved doing had been killed by my limiting beliefs and fears. I had become a passion killer!

Fast forward about three years, my life and everything that came along with it was still going on as usual. I was faithfully going to work at the schoolhouse. I was structured, organized, and systematic in all I did. When you walked into my classroom, you walked in to order.

But one February, also nationally recognized as Black History Month, changed my life. It was the moment I realized that I was a change agent, a history maker my own doggone self! But my emancipation did not happen without casualties.

I remember it like it was yesterday. It began with a simple trip to the teachers' workroom. As I was using the copy machine, my co-workers walked in. We began talking about our Black History event the night before. Even though I was not in attendance at the program, I was the teacher who was the creative mind behind what the sixth graders did.

There were unfavorable comments made about the performance itself. To be honest I can't remember exactly what was said. What I do remember is that, from that point on, all of my senses were heightened. I saw, felt, and heard every thing. Before that two-minute conversation in the workroom, I was numb inside, simply existing. I had awakened like a sleeping giant. Now let me make it clear, at that point I didn't realize I had been sleep. I did not know that simple conversation was the catalyst God was using to move me into destiny.

No longer sleep, now I was aware that I was trapped in a life I no longer wanted. I was suffocating in that classroom because I felt stifled. I was frustrated because I was uncomfortable, but that was all I had so what was I to do? To be honest I didn't know what was happening, all I knew was that I wanted more.

There were many days I cried on the inside. Living an unfulfilled life doing what I was called to do was like living in hell. Torment, that's what it felt like. I began expressing a desire to do something else, maybe even go to another school. Something had to give. I knew my students would eventually, if not already, be affected.

Fast forward a couple a years, things only got worse. Uncomfortable, out of sorts, out of place, misfit, resentful, paranoid, broken relationships, unfulfilled, trapped, jealousy, envy, disappointment, helplessness, doubt, uncertainty, depression, unproductive, ineffective, unintentional, zombie, lifeless, just existing, no direction.

"GOD COME TO MY RESCUE I NEED YOU!!!" I cried out to the only One I thought would listen and had an answer to my problem.

If I woke up one more morning not being satisfied with my life, I was going to literally lose my mind. Losing "it" was what really scared me the most. It was my sanity, my relationships, my husband, my finances, my intimacy with GOD, my job, but most of all, my ability to dream.

I had lost the dreamer in me. She died somewhere between the teacher's lounge and the cafeteria, so I settled myself in my classroom. Mediocrity had invaded the heart of a champion. The only thing left to do was to retreat or die, or in this case, they were one in the same.

Depression is real and I had been fighting it since 2002, and now here it was 2012 and I wasn't sure if I could go any further. I knew what a functioning alcoholic's life must have felt like. I was functioning in a state of depression.

Whoa I just said that out loud, Jesus help me!

I was in a state of depression. The fight in me was about to fizzle. I could not go back into that classroom and pretend that I was happy and satisfied. I wasn't. I needed more, not sure what "more" was, but I longed for it like an asthmatic longed for air. I wasn't a great teacher. I had been damaged.

Damaged teachers don't do their students any good. I had been giving my students my best, but in a broken state. So Johnny was given my best heartache; Sally my best disappointment; Mary my broken pieces; all wrapped up in mediocrity and presented as educating my students.

Honestly, for a long time I thought I was doing some great teaching, and that was the biggest lie I ever told myself. I was lucky enough to be an over-achiever, but I couldn't help but wonder what student missed out on their break-through because of my breakdown. I was broken and didn't even know it.

How many of you are in a broken state, trying to fix everything around you, but nothing that is in you?

Every day I went in to work, but at that point it was a religious act. My calling had taken a back seat to low teacher morale caused by years of low pay and even lower appreciation. It was very hard to teach when you were barely making it to your next paycheck, you had so much paperwork to complete, programs to implement, and no consistent professional development to help you implement the new program.

No one can change my mind on this: I think all teachers should make a minimum of $100,000 a year, not including health insurance, and each of us should receive at least $300 in food stamps. Yes I said it! We should get food stamps!

Even though I was out of touch with my friends and especially my co- workers, I turned to GOD. Relationship matters to me. Slowly relational unity was dissipating. When I realized that I couldn't trust the people whom I worked with and called friends, I knew it was time for GOD to intervene.

I would walk up on conversations about me. I had been alienated. And my principal who once respected me no longer held me in high regard. Of course it was all them, right? None of it was the fact that I was out of place, out of order, and most of all, just being plain ole disobedient.

I realized disobedience started the war, put me in the hell I was in, and was carrying me straight to the psyche ward if I didn't stop the madness. My only recourse was to walk away. Actually it was perfect timing because the sixth grade was moving to the middle school, and I taught sixth grade. It was time for me to escape. My coworkers/friends didn't like me, my principal seemed to be irritated by me, so why not move with the sixth grade to the middle school? It would be a change of environment, a fresh start. So I did just that! Problem solved!

Walking into my new classroom gave me the jump start to get going again. I was super excited about being a part of a school that the community deemed a lost cause. I put on my cape and Vicki to the rescue!

I had a reason to be great. God placed me there so I could support a team of terrific educators and change the trajectory of the school. They hyped us up. We were told that sixth grade was the missing piece. We were hand-picked and considered to be the best in the system. To me, those were fighting words, but fighting in a good way. If I was considered the best, I was going to be the best, and I was going to fight whatever to be just that. Waking up excited to be going to work was refreshing. My problems were over, I just needed a new environment and to be around new people. Problem solved.

For a while I was in love. I loved my administration, the entire faculty and staff. The sixth grade team was the dream team. We loved, respected, and genuinely liked each other. We functioned as one unit. Finally I got back what I missed most of all, unity.

As educators we can't do it alone. If you want to experience success, you must function as a team. Success is truly a team support. With an awesome administrator and grade level team, not to mention just being in a new environment was refreshing. I know I said that before, but that was a feeling I remember the most about that time in my life.

What could go wrong when you work with such a great group of people? Everything if you are still not doing the right things, in the right order, at the right time. As a result, frustration crept back, depression started rearing its ugly head, and discontentment pounced on me panther-like as if I were its prey. This time around I could not deny that my life was spinning out of control. I was sick, and putting a band-aid over this dis-ease wasn't going to work. Not this time.

This time around, with even more intensity, depression tried to take me out. It is funny though that I never once considered going to the doctor, mainly because I did not want anything like that in my medical records. I was also an insurance producer, so I knew how that would affect my life insurance.

I remember talking to a friend who had a nervous breakdown. I told her that I felt like it just may happen to me. I also talked to a family member and shared with her that I had to fight depression. She said, "At some point I think we all have to fight it; and that if we let ourselves go, we would all be in the looney bin." Her words comforted me. For some strange reason, that brought me solace, but more importantly it was the genesis of my turnaround.

As teachers we teach our students strategies to help with comprehension. Well the truth is, I had to use some of those same strategies to comprehend what was going on in my life and get back on track. Teachers must be life-long learners. Therefore I took time and thought about what I really wanted in life and what would make me happy. I guess you can say I 'brain-stormed'.

I went back to my childhood and thought on the times that brought me joy. My happiest thoughts weren't necessarily events that I remembered, but snippets of me encouraging people or rooting for the underdog. In its simplest, purest form, my memories of helping people changed my life forever. No longer could I ignore it. God, in all of His splendor, faithfulness, mercy, and grace allowed me to see my purpose in the midst of darkness.

So what was I to do with that epiphany? So what I loved encouraging and helping people? I was a motivator, but what did that really mean in the scheme of things? How was knowing that going to help me get back to me, and get back to teaching those children who deserved me at 100% every single day?

The truth and nothing but the truth, many days we may give all we have to give, but that "all" is us performing at 60%. No matter what state we're in mentally, physically, or emotionally, our students deserve the other 40%. Great teachers are never satisfied.

Anyway, it was in my nature to encourage and motivate. Even on my worst day, I could encourage someone else to go and do some amazing things. As a matter of fact, many friends own businesses now because I encouraged them to go after their dreams. However, as an educator who was there to encourage me? I definitely was not getting it when I walked in the school house. What do you do when the encourager needs encouraging?

I found myself desperately needing to do something... anything... other than teach. Grasping for anything that resembled better and more, I joined a financial services company as an independent consultant. Oh my goodness! This decision was exactly what I needed. I was making great money, meeting new people, and sharing information with families that changed their lives.

Everything was going well but I still felt stuck. I still felt like God wanted me doing more. Things weren't getting better, they were only getting worse.

The thing I loved doing the most was what I now dreaded doing. Routinely, I would get up at 4 o'clock in the morning to start my day with prayer and meditation. Slowly 4 o'clock turned into 5 o'clock, that turned into 5:30 a.m. Eventually I did not want to get up at all.

Get up for what? Nothing I seemed to do was making a difference. The children didn't seem to be understanding. I was an English Language Arts (ELA) teacher, so my job was extremely difficult. Many of my students were performing below grade level. The parents wanted teachers to just give the students passing grades. As a matter of fact, the parents needed to adjust more to middle school than their child.

Something had to give. I didn't want to go in to work, and I had absolutely no more sick days left to take off. Something had to change. Laying in the bed was not the answer, that much I knew.

Out of nowhere, I remembered my mother's famous words to me as a child, "Rise and shine, rise even if you don't shine." At first it didn't mean anything. I really didn't understand why I couldn't get those annoying, yet comforting, words out my mind.

Days went by and those words were still playing in my head like a broken record. Each day that I didn't want to get up. Each day that I didn't know my purpose, I would hear my mom's words. One day those words changed my life and propelled me into my destiny. My mom was Maxine Johnson. That mother of four I talked about at the beginning of this chapter.

Before that dark moment of my life, *Rise and shine, rise even if you don't shine*, was just a song my mom sung to wake up my siblings and me. I simply thought it was a song to wake us up and have us ready for school on time. But now, decades later, God had shown me what it truly meant.

The truth is, that song was God's way of ever so sweetly giving me directions on how to start my day. You see, God knew it would be a time when I would wake up with no intentions. Thinking about it today, He knew I would be frustrated, uncomfortable, and unfulfilled. He knew that I would have to one day just *Rise and shine, rise even if I didn't shine*.

You see, as educators there will be many days that you are not going to want to walk through that door and teach. But it is at that very instance that you have to rise. Rising is not just physically getting up. That was my epiphany: Rising was more so a mental and a heart action, than it was a physical one.

More than anything I needed to rise. I needed to do what I was called to do even in my moments of despair. Taking action even in despair determined my success in and out of the classroom.

You will not know everything as an educator, but it doesn't mean you stand still or stay stuck.

When my purpose was cloudy, I became frustrated and everything was uncomfortable. I began to sink instead of rise.

We must show up no matter what!

In my despair, I stopped showing up. Yes I clocked in everyday but my best didn't clock in with me. I sunk into my situation instead of rising up from it.

Some sort of way we cannot allow our lives to get so overwhelmed that we settle for half-best and mediocrity. The answer to your despair is to rise.

I began this chapter by sharing with you how unfulfilled I was, and how I let it get out of hand. What I realized was that I needed to do more.

Sometimes as educators it is not that we are doing too much but that we aren't doing enough of the right thing. I found myself spending 90% of my time doing only 10% of what I needed to be doing. No one did it but me.

No one is keeping you trapped. No one is keeping you from rising. No one is keeping you from being the best version of yourself but you. Don't be like I was for at least five years. I had trapped myself in my classroom. Yes, I held myself hostage. My classroom was my holding cell.

Sadly I know that there are so many other teachers out there that have limited their passion to the confines of their classroom.

Passion is not to be limited, and if so, it slowly kills as a way to survive.

Rise my fellow educators... Rise! Go and be the great men and women you are. Don't limit your gifts to just the classroom. If you desire to do something in addition to teaching, don't let anyone make you feel guilty.

Wanting to do something in addition to teaching isn't adulterous. You are not cheating on your students or school. There were co-workers who, with much love, told me not to be hard on myself, that it was OK to feel unfulfilled, and I just needed to sit still and it would pass. They meant no harm but it wasn't the best advice for me. Once I began to reach beyond those four walls, I started showing up within those four walls. You must do the same!

I don't know what caused your fall, for me it was settling for making a difference only within the four walls of my classroom. Your fall may be bad classroom management, no organization, procrastination, low self-esteem, stinking thinking and the list can go on and on. No matter what, I want you to Rise.

There will be times when the last place you want to be is at work in that classroom, but you cannot focus on you. You must look beyond your feelings and think about the lives that have been assigned to you.

My rise came when God told me that I forgot who I am to serve. My response was, "God I know I am to serve You." But God clearly told me that I was to serve those students. He told me that in order to go beyond where I was, I would have to change my perception of my students. He said each and every day I would have to show up to serve my students. All I could say was Whoa and Wow. Another Aha moment with God.

So what did I do? I served those students each and every day! When things began to unravel, you know things like excessive paperwork, low test scores, undervalued, lack of training and resources, I held on to my mother's words: Rise and shine, rise even if you don't shine.

Every time I willed myself to rise, I allowed the best of me to show up. Showing up for me was the Shine my mom talked about. She never separated the two. She always said rise and shine. She knew that if I could look up, I could get up. She knew that in my rising, my light would be revealed for all to see.

Educators your shine is not for you but for those students, parents, and fellow educators that are in darkness. Your light illuminates the paths of others. I know you thought it was about you... it isn't.

Having experienced some tumultuous times in my 20 years of teaching, I can truly say that the good outweigh the bad. Not many are called to such a responsibility as us teachers, so not many understand us... and that can truly be a lonely place. Remember to Rise and shine, rise even if you don't shine.

Dr. Ragan Brown

I'm Done, I Quit, It's Over

I'm done! This was the second consecutive year I convinced myself that leaving the profession of teaching was my only option. At this point, I had nothing else to lose. The hard part was figuring out what was I going to do at this crossroads in my life? Do I take a year off? Do I start a new career?

"It's time," I muttered.

My fractured, bruised, and broken mind didn't believe my words. My life as an educator felt... Empty. Thoughts of how I was designed and created to teach, encourage, and activate were no longer in existence.

Over the course of nine years, if given a report card or progress note, I would have been retained.

I failed at my relationships. I lost self-control. I failed miserably at work-life balance. I lost hope. I failed at taking opportunities. I lost drive. I failed at my passion for encouraging. I lost my zest for teaching. I failed at my purpose. I failed me.

How did this happen? Why did it happen? How did it get this far? Is this really what I signed up for...

Imagine a leech draining the blood from my skin, I felt like teaching absorbed the life out of me. My thoughts were ruthless, hopeless, and I began to spiral down a destructive emotional path. Maybe I cared too much.

Eventually, that started fading because what I thought helped to define me, contributed to dismantling me. As much I knew I was designed to be and that I was designed for greatness, I struggled with understanding my professional worth as an educator.

The truth is...

If I am responsible for contributing to the formation and advancement of a nation, then why do I feel less than? After a while, I didn't believe it. I was just a teacher. I never asked to be placed on a pedestal, I never asked for fame. The one and only request was respect for my profession.

When did the perception of teachers change? We're just babysitters, right? We only work nine months, right? We play games with kids all day, right? Teachers shouldn't voice their concerns, right? After all, it's not so bad.

The whole truth is, many people in various professions couldn't walk a day in a teacher's shoes. Thankfully, there are many people who appreciate the professional worth of a teacher. However, that group of individuals who truly don't respect teachers, contribute to the deterioration of the teacher.

How did this demise begin...

Honestly, I didn't always feel this way. Like most new teachers, I was over zealous about my classroom theme and getting all of my curriculum material posted. It was official, I was a sixth grade English Language Arts teacher ready to help shape the minds of our future educators, lawyers, doctors, engineers, business professionals, entrepreneurs, technology professionals, and all other professionals.

We all know them: the "Teacher of the Year", the teacher who gets routine observations from new teachers, the teacher who teaches a concept to students who never forget, the teacher who gets a visit from former students reminding her of how they impacted a life, the teacher who is asked to serve on every decision-making committee, a member of multiple Professional Learning Communities (PLC), the teacher who receives note after note, the teacher whose class is the academic party spot because kids are literally rocking and rolling while learning. We know them!

That first year of teaching brought so many joys, from setting up my classroom, to helping to get students' scores higher on the great standardize tests. In the midst of it all, I had so many challenges that I didn't expect in an elementary school.

I thought I had all my routines in place, but what I didn't realize is that I couldn't control how the outside environmental factors would influence the tone of my classroom. That first year, I had elementary students involved in gangs, drugs, and so many other unbelievable acts. That same year I also experienced harassment from a student. As much as I have tried to block it out, it somehow remained a fixture in my mind.

This particular student was older than most of my students in sixth grade. He would constantly make sexual comments to me and about me to the other male students. He would draw graphic pictures which represented me that were inappropriate. Then one day, he was so angry for getting detention, he told other students that he would perform some inappropriate and violent acts on me if I followed through with the after school consequence. This was truly unimaginable and I didn't realize just how much it upset me. I immediately and constantly reported all of his harassment but this last time was the straw that broke the camel's back. Due to his repeated sexual harassment, he was transferred to the alternative school for the remainder of the school year. Although, it was a tough emotional year, my resiliency kicked in and I continued to teach my heart out.

The honeymoon second year of teaching was a bumpy ride, but I had a rhythm. My classroom management was in order, students were in engaged in the learning process, and I was happy in my relationships with family, friends, and my long-time boyfriend.

My challenge was reaching students who had multiple learning differences. As an enthusiastic fairly new teacher, I constantly researched academic accommodations and made the necessary provisions and modifications to ensure every student experienced growth. This was when the late nights began. By the end of the school year, I was not only a certified teacher, but a certified workaholic. Work was so addictive and demanding that I neglected everything in my path. Ultimately it felt like I failed at everything, including my relationship with the man I thought would one day be my husband.

Then, just like toddlers in their terrible threes, my third year of teaching resembled torture. Every other day I was either interrupted by a behavior issue or called an unthinkable name by students (stupid, dumbass, or every English and Spanish swear word). For the most part, my students were engaged but they challenged my patience and salvation.

I had several alpha males in that class and they were determined to break me. I never let them see me break a sweat but that was the year my skin became tougher. The anger that my students displayed carried over into my personal encounters with family members. I would possibly describe myself as a tyrant back then. Looking back, I wouldn't want to be in my own company either. That was the year I lost self-control.

After some much needed self-reflection during the summer, I was emotionally recharged and equipped with strategies, organizers, SMART goals, interventions, and management to begin the new school year.

To my surprise, it worked! Years 4 and 5 were probably a few of my best years. Entering my fourth year of teaching, I felt like a Superhero (that may have been the theme for my class that year). Ready to tackle the world, I enrolled in graduate school to begin coursework towards my PhD in Child Development, in effort to further understand children and how life experiences influenced their behaviors.

I also began presenting staff development and participating on various committees through my school district. I was literally rocking and rolling when year five began. Soon, I took on so many projects that I didn't realize how much time I dedicated to career advancement, my personal education journey, and my quest to be an outstanding teacher. My students were doing well and I was at the peak of my career in education. But I failed miserably at work-life balance and the sad part was, I had lost those years before and had just realized it.

As hard as I worked, I often felt like I wasn't going anywhere. Have you ever felt pigeon holed, or like a caged bird? Soon, I lost hope.

Opportunities that would advance me elsewhere surfaced and I tried to take advantage sometimes. Most of the time I didn't though. I was now at the point where I felt less than. I began to experience a professional drought. I failed at taking opportunities.

The wonder years...

The next few years were the wonder years and truly a blur. I already felt that my job as an educator wasn't important. It didn't help when other professionals asked why are you teaching and you know it doesn't pay well.

My thoughts were tainted. Other factors contributed to those foggy years, I lost several coworkers due to passing away or grave illnesses. I couldn't help but wonder if I was next. Thinking to myself often will the stress of the job over power me. It was already tough being a teacher with Attention Deficit Hyperactivity Disorder (ADHD), but when you throw anxiety into the equation, that is one formula you don't want to mix! As I attempted to release some of the pressures, in the process, I lost drive.

And now, the thrill was gone. No longer did I have the energy to put into the lesson plans for my students. I think I was going through the motions. Although the students learned and exceeded expectations, I knew wholeheartedly that I did not give it my all in the classroom.

And knowing that hurt me to the core. I failed at my passion for encouraging. I toyed with the idea again of leaving, but I didn't feel as though I could contribute anywhere else in the world.

As I prepared to complete my coursework for my PhD program, I still could not believe that there was more that I could give. Looking back, my mind was literally playing tricks on me. Thankfully, this did not impact the students. That spring I teetered with the idea of leaving the profession. I started the process of my dissertation and literally could not remain focused.

I applied for a position as a Campus Reading Specialist, hoping that I would be afforded a little more time to work on advancing my students without the additional stressors of being a classroom teacher. I got the position and hit the ground running the following year. My goal was to help teachers present reading lessons in more effective and engaging ways. In addition, I would assist teachers with mini lessons for small groups of students based on analyzed data.

This new position was fun for a little while until old habits quickly resurfaced. Like previous years, I would remain at work until 8:00 pm and many nights were 9:30 pm. I thought for sure the new position would change my attitude. I was wrong.

I broke.

I failed me.

I'm done...

So I sat, in my office alone on that final day of the school year and thought about my life. The truth is I poured my entire heart, soul, sweat, and tears without expecting anything. What felt like a ton of bricks hitting me, I realized I was torn, confused, and lost. I had let the emotional pressure of my job rule my life and I no longer enjoyed the profession. It was truly self-sabotage. For over nine years, I had lived in organized chaos.

Something had to change...

I literally ran away from teaching. I packed up my car and went home to Louisiana, and I took a break. That wasn't the regular return home for the summer. That summer was different. I resigned and focused on my abandoned dissertation for the PhD program. I told myself I would never go back to teaching.

Through constant communication with God, I profusely cried out to Him and asked for direction. I listened intently and I was ordered to return to teaching with the condition of taking a full year off to breathe. God whispered to me that there was more work that was required of me in the classroom and in the field of education.

The truth is I craved it, I was addicted to teaching and learning new content to teach to my students. I never stopped loving teaching. I only hated who I became because of the lack of self-care, and the lack of knowing and owning my professional worth.

From destruction to reconstruction...

I wrote letters to myself to get myself out of that rut. I no longer wanted to be held captive to negativity towards a profession that I knew contributed to making a difference in this world. I took charge and did not allow opinions and societal views of the teaching profession overwhelm me. I had to constantly study and work on myself to develop a new love for my profession.

In a year, I had come a long way, and I plan to return to teaching to further develop my craft, to advocate for our youth, to do the research, to teach and mentor teachers, and to continue to assist in building a nation. I have a responsibility.

As I prepare for my second career as a teacher, I feel restored and renewed. This time, I am going back to the basics. I revisited my journals over the years that I felt the happiest in my career. The exact same thing that my students required of me, is the same thing that rejuvenated my drive for teaching. In order for me to be the best teacher to our future, it is imperative that I am the best teacher to myself. It is important for me to require realistic expectations of myself. Going forward, I plan to implement everything that I instill in my students. From now on, I would practice what I teach.

Learning Objectives (by the end of each school year):

- I will practice positive self-talk.
- I will nourish my body with healthy meals, liquids, thoughts, and movements.
- I will take time to spend with family and friends.
- I will find new ways to advance in my career.

- I will embed times to disconnect and decompress.
- I will master work-life balance.
- My passion for teaching will be deeper and my purpose will become clearer.
- I will not be emotionally done with my profession.

Am I done? No! This is only the beginning.

The Whole Truth & Nothing But the Truth, So Help Me Teachers!

The Mediocre Teacher

All I'd ever wanted to be was a teacher. I can't remember ever even considering another profession. It wasn't that I liked all teachers. In elementary school, of course, but as I got older, I realized that they weren't all good. It was my love of school and learning that made me want to be a teacher. A good one at that. One who loved her subject, students, and school. For several years, I was that teacher.

During the first half of my teaching career, my friends thought I was absolutely crazy to be so in love with a profession that did not love me back. No one could understand how working with sometimes apathetic and occasionally disrespectful teenagers could be anyone's dream job; but for me it was. I was excited to go to work each day. I couldn't wait to try a new lesson or set up a cool lab experiment. There were several students that I looked forward to seeing each day. I couldn't wait to hear what they had to say or laugh at their jokes.

There was absolutely nothing at the time that could change my mind about teaching. I'd earned my Master's degree within my first two years and I had plans of pursuing a doctoral degree. I knew that I needed to make money in order to support my love of travel, so I knew I needed a higher degree.

Although I worked in other areas of education seasonally, I had no intentions of leaving the profession. EVER. However, a series of events led me to a point where I could barely stand to enter a classroom daily.

I'd gone from having keys and the security code to my school building--because I'd arrive so early, stay so late, and was known for showing up on the weekends--to a teacher who sat in her car until the very last minute before entering the building. I became a teacher who dreaded creating lesson plans, although I'd previously lived for creating dynamic and engaging lessons! I became a teacher who stopped grading papers, when in the past, I'd been the very same teacher who graded everything the same day it was submitted and returned it to students the following day!

I was a teacher who was frustrated, tired, and uninspired. I still loved the art of teaching, but I admired nothing about the work attached to being a teacher. I still got excited with new ideas for ways to engage my students, but I was no longer willing to make those experiences happen consistently. I was doing just enough to make it through each day. I was in survival mode. I had become a mediocre teacher.

A mediocre teacher is one who is an overall GREAT teacher, who LOVES teaching; but also HATES going to work.

I think I should explain this mediocrity thing a little more. You see, at no point was I a teacher who lacked talent, passion, or ability to perform in excellence each day. In fact, at my core, that was still my desire. Although I was functioning in survival mode, I truly did want to give my all.

I'd go to bed every night promising that I'd get back on track the next day, but when the new day arrived, I found myself settling all over again.

So, how, exactly, does this happen? How does a teacher become a mediocre teacher?

In my case, there were a series of events that led to my mediocrity. The first was my decision to leave a school and position that I absolutely loved. I had become quite content and highly effective in that particular school. I loved the students and they loved me. I was teaching my favorite subject and I was the advisor of one of the most important extracurricular activities in the building.

I'd developed a system that was working well and anyone with eyes could see that I was excited about doing my job. Of course, there was a downside to everything. While I was very happy in my position, I was also an ambitious person.

I'd started my doctoral program and had goals of moving up one day. I knew that there was no way I was ever leaving the classroom working for the school district that I loved so much. For one, there were few leaders of color and even less female leaders of color.

I was not well-connected beyond my school building. In fact, inside of my building, my teaching methods, although all research-based, were often frowned upon by many teachers because they were not the typical.

For example, I was doing standards-based grading before it was a "thing". My assignments and assessments measured one standard at a time, and I allowed students to retake the portions that they did not master after attending a tutorial session, as many times as necessary until they were able to show mastery. Can you say *proficiency scales?*

I can recall the other teachers in my department complaining that their students expected the same, but that they did not agree with this teaching method. They would also complain that I conducted too many labs which prompted their students to request more labs than they had the time, energy, or interest in conducting.

I invited parents into my classroom to help evaluate presentations, participate in labs, or just observe. No one else was doing that. I would say that I was tolerated by my colleagues, but not very well liked due to my unwillingness to go along with the status quo.

In spite of my love for the school, students, and parents, I longed to be more than a classroom teacher. I wanted to impact the practice of other teachers. I felt that if I could just share these practices – which, by the way were getting great results – I could, in turn, impact more students. I knew that if I wanted to do this, I'd have to go somewhere else.

As fate would have it, I learned of a school that seemed to be a great fit for my teaching style and by chance met a member of the administrative team of that school shortly thereafter. To me, those were all signs that my opportunity for professional growth was presenting itself.

Long story short, I attended the school's job fair, completed two rounds of interviews, and was offered a position. Not just a teaching position, but the position of department chair. I wouldn't just be the department chair, but I would also develop the curriculum for the high school division that would soon be added. That was my chance to advance, indeed!

Little did I know, the decision to leave a school and position that I loved would be the first in a series of decisions that landed me in the mediocrity trap! Almost immediately after joining the faculty at the new school, I knew it was not for me. The culture did not align with my beliefs, the workload was unrealistic, and the administration could not be trusted.

And, please, let's not talk about the students. The students were the absolute worst I'd ever had. I could not relate to them and they felt no connection to me. I didn't receive any of the resources that had been promised to me in my interviews. Quite contrary, I was expected to use my own money to purchase materials and equipment for my classes!

It was clear that I made a huge mistake and I began to see a drastic change in my practice almost instantly. I was no longer getting to work early or staying late. I was not on fire to implement new lessons or labs. I didn't look forward to seeing certain students or laughing at their jokes. I arrived at work just in time, I left as soon as I could, and I was no-nonsense with the students.

I knew that I would not be returning the next school year, regardless of how they tried to dress up the position. Thankfully, my disdain for the school, its students, and its administration was mutual. For the first time in my life, I was fired from a job and I was not the least bit sad about it. I was actually relieved that I would not have to spend another precious minute of life in that building, with those kids, and that administration. I could move on and get back to the type of school and students that I loved...or so I thought.

Unfortunately, my newfound freedom lasted a bit longer that I desired. I interviewed everywhere. I mean, everywhere, but I could not get a job. Now, that was something new for me. Up until that point, I had never interviewed for a job without receiving an offer! What was I going to do? I needed a job and I still wanted to teach!

Eventually, I landed a position. I just knew that I would love my new school and students as much as I'd loved those at my previous school. Again, I was wrong.

While this new school shared many demographic characteristics as my old school, it was by no means the same type of school. I started with the intention of getting back into my old habits of excellence, but reality quickly set in.

Once again, I did not love the school, the students, or the administration. Despite this, I tried my best to be the best that I knew how to be. Besides, my reputation was on the line and I didn't want to be known as a lazy teacher.

I fell into my old routine of planning engaging, hands-on lessons, arriving to work early, and providing frequent feedback. I did not get back into the routine of staying late. I was completely over that part. I was able to keep this up for the first two years in this new school. Around the third year, I could feel myself slipping again.

I failed to mention a huge factor that also contributed to my mediocrity: being diagnosed with Lupus. Lupus is an autoimmune disease that takes place when your body's immune system attacks its own tissues and organs, which causes excruciating pain.

Up until that point, my lupus had not had a profound impact on my ability to teach; but throw in the fact that while I was unemployed my home went into foreclosure, I'd been in a relationship that turned physically abusive, had to move into a one-bedroom apartment with my mother, and was desperately fighting with the college to grant me more time to complete my doctoral degree, and you've got the perfect recipe for lupus to run rampant!

I was always tired, always in pain, and always stressed out. I couldn't do a good job every day, regardless of the time I arrived or left school. My body just couldn't keep up with the demand and I found myself barely able to make it through each day.

Enthusiasm turned into dread. Creativity became unimaginative lesson planning. Ambition turned into survival. I was doing just enough to get by each day. There was nothing special about my classes or me. I was just another teacher. A mediocre teacher.

I still loved the idea of teaching, but I absolutely hated going to work and there was nothing I could do about it. I was already earning significantly less than I had in previous years and my lupus was so out of control that there was no way I could be without insurance.

I had nothing left to give to my students. I knew I had no business working – for their sake or mine – but I simply could not quit. So I continued on this path of mediocrity for another two years.

Don't get me wrong. I wasn't mediocre every day for two years straight. I had my moments.

Some days, even weeks, I'd be my old self: delivering innovative lessons with the excitement of a brand-new teacher, happy to see my students, and serving on committees to help improve the school. Those times, however, did not last. As much as I wanted to stay on the right track, on the path of excellence, I could not keep it up for longer than three to four weeks at a time. I certainly wanted to, but my body just wouldn't cooperate. I was completely miserable and I knew that something would have to change.

Despite the challenges, I was able to finally complete my doctoral degree. Accomplishing that goal seemed to re-ignite a spark in me to take control of my situation.

So, yet again, I started the job search. This time, to find a school that really fit my needs and personality. This time, I'd look for a position teaching my favorite subject to the demographic with which I'd previously had the most success. I'd also only apply in districts that paid the amount of money that I desired and deserved to make. This time, I'd be completely honest with myself and I wouldn't cut any corners in creating the ideal situation for me to be the most effective teacher I could possibly be. I was determined to escape the mediocrity trap!

In the last teaching position I held, I finally had it all again. I was teaching a subject that I loved. This made it fun! I had an awesome administrative staff. This made it easier to do my job. I had students that I looked forward to seeing each day. Everything had come full circle.

I was nominated for several district-level committees and supplemental assignments. The opportunity to advance was realistic and I was earning an amount of money that I felt was fair for the amount of work I was required to do.

I began to create again. I developed unique teaching methods that were effective in reaching unmotivated students or students who lacked some of the basic pre-requisite skills required for the courses that I taught. I started to present at conferences and was called upon to conduct trainings.

I escaped mediocrity! I was no longer a mediocre teacher! After several years of doing just enough to get by, I had rediscovered everything I loved about teaching.

The Whole Truth & Nothing But the Truth, So Help Me Teachers!

Nicole Brown-Horston

In Loving Memory of Grandma

"You can lead a horse to water, but you can't make him drink. You can lead a student to knowledge, but you can't make him think."

– Nicole Brown-Horston

Growing up, I always helped my mother take care of my grandmother. My grandparents were born in 1913, so I never truly understood the hardships that my grandparents faced. After my grandfather died, I became my grandmother's trusted companion. This 5'3" woman could manage a household and knew how much money she had down to the cent.

One day my mother had already left for work and I needed a permission slip signed for school. I handed the paper to my grandmother to read. In the beginning, I thought that she was genuinely concerned with me going on the field trip because she asked me a lot of questions about what the paper was for. Finally, it hit me like a ton of bricks--my grandmother couldn't read. I continued to answer her questions and she signed the paper for me. I put it in my book bag and acted as if the event never happened.

The next day when I was in school, I asked the Librarian if she could help me find a beginner's reading book because I wanted to help someone learn how to read. She gave me a handful of books to choose from. For the remainder of that day, I couldn't wait to get home from school to share my surprise with my grandmother.

When the bell rang, I had to wait for my younger sister and two cousins because we always had to walk home together. As we approached our street, I ran as fast as I could to the front porch.

There, my grandmother stood on the last step so she could see us as we approached the house. I ran up to her, grabbed her down towards me and whispered, "I have a secret that I want to share with you when we get into the house." That little secret shaped my purpose because I taught my grandmother how to read.

My grandmother wanted me to become a nurse, but I always knew I was created to be an Educator. When I earned my Bachelor's degree, I can remember leaving the stage at The Ohio State University ready to change the world. Inside was that same burning inferno that I had with my grandmother, and I had no doubt that I was going to be the best educator ever.

When I received my first assignment in the classroom, my initial feelings were quickly shattered. You see, all of the teaching and learning theories that I had acquired in college never equipped me to deal with students who were broken. Students who were behind in learning came to school unprepared and a disruption to the learning environment.

Grappling with these issues and the number of students I had, I asked myself was this something that I wanted to get involved with, and how would I be able to teach each child in order to reach them. It was painfully obvious by the second day of class that teaching from the book would not impact them as much as teaching from the heart.

As I sat at my desk after the end of my first week, I knew I had to come up with a game plan fast. Pondering, I played out all of the scenarios that really stood out to me throughout the week and I soon found a pattern of behavior in each of them. There were common themes in those students who were a disruption and those who were behind.

I did something that I never thought I would do--I spent the entire weekend calling each of the parents whose children were a problem and I asked for a home visit. Now, this wasn't something that middle school teachers were customary to do, but I wanted to understand their environment, through their lens. I wanted to know what was their home life like? Their parents? Siblings? Did their parents work late and they had no one available when they came home from school, also referred to as Latchkey kids?

During the initial phase, I asked myself, "Are you able to empathize with each of their situations without judgment enough to really reach them?"

In our wonderful world of education, I have found that we would much rather overburden teachers by having them aggregate data which is never used for improvement. Then also blame the lack of parental support and other factors to reinforce false notions of inferiority to explain why our students aren't making gains, why they aren't being equipped with what they need to graduate, why they aren't being accepted into colleges and ultimately, why they aren't a productive member of society.

In order for this paradigm shift to really make a difference in the educational system, we must realize that all students need an Individualized Education Plan that addresses them as an individual and celebrates their gifts and talents.

The Whole Truth & Nothing But the Truth, So Help Me Teachers!

A paradigm shift is an important change that happens when the usual way of thinking about or doing something is replaced by new ideas to be tried, eventually leading to a new paradigm (a different way of thinking). My home visits were when the paradigm shift began to take form in my classroom. In my case, it was my students' inability to grasp grade-level concepts because of old habits. I was determined, after delving into their backstories, to eliminate every barrier to learning that was within my power in order to strengthen their educational experience.

Needless to say that after those phone calls and meetings, my perspectives changed and I learned an enduring lesson that has been with me throughout my career. I began to tell my students that attending school was like being at their job. Their grades were equivalent to their paychecks.

I also started incorporating character education along with the mandated lessons. Meaning, I made real-life applications to each of their lessons in order to equip them with high self-esteem, relationship skills and how to deal with difficult tasks. We began each day with affirmations and short-term goals, and we ended the day with one thing that we would improve upon tomorrow.

I did whatever it took to put their best interests at the forefront. This wasn't an easy task and at the end of the day, my health paid the ultimate price.

I spent countless hours tracking my students and their progress which resulted in many sleepless nights, improper eating habits and being mentally and physically drained. It was worth it. Like my grandmother, my students began to excel, even the most vulnerable ones.

The Whole Truth & Nothing But the Truth, So Help Me Teachers!

Tamika L. Blythers

I Made A Vow

Somewhere along the way the lines had been blurred as to the definition of a teacher, not to mention our duties and responsibilities. I often wondered why the teacher is a part of the five-fold ministry in the Bible. After two decades in the classroom, I now understand that for nine months the teacher lives in the 'basement confessional' of every student. Each child presenting their sterile, perfected image while dragging dirty, concealed laundry to unload and deposit into the teacher's life for the next nine months. Conception has begun.

We deal with and listen to students' silent, yet screaming confessions about the torment of depression, illnesses, goals, visions, deflated self-esteem, no self-pride, loneliness, jealousy, mental, physical, or sexual abuse, abandonment, bipolar disorders, fear, worry, anxiety, homelessness, hunger, lice, bedbugs, narcissism, dyslexia, Oppositional Defiant Disorder (ODD), Attention-Deficit Disorder (ADD), Attention-Deficit Hyperactivity Disorder (ADHD), gender identification, rejection, sociopathic, psychopathic, and a mountain of other issues children carry and toss at our feet.

We are confined to that basement battle for three quarters, and still have to balance and maintain our own lives in the midst of the mess dumped on the educational threshing floor.

Welcome to "The Window". This is the truth, my realistic truth. I've had a countless number of individuals asking me how do I teach year after year. They wonder, even marvel at the sheer idea of a teacher being confined or sentenced to the profession of teaching, knowing we are like "spiritual hazmat" specialists dealing with students' unlimited issues.

What do you do when there are at least twenty-five students in the classroom? I say apply "The Window" perspective. It's a perspective that I've created to handle issues and actions. Within the window of teaching time, expect the best, worse, and everything in between. Let nothing that students say or do surprise you or catch you off guard.

Never get offended because the window of time to teach that child will not last forever. The teacher's saving grace is they have nine months with them, but the parents have at least nineteen more years with students. It's all about staying focused and keeping "The Window" perspective.

My goal is to teach the teacher how to preserve their livelihood and sanity. Calm down...... Breathe...... we'll get through this.

Teachers have to remember that they are living in the confessionals of the students, and their responsibility is to make a choice to either evangelize or antagonize, insult or inspire. The students' permanent folders provide an inside scoop into their lives and every single thing that they've encountered. It also gives us a brief snapshot and guides us to which angle to cut and slice into the classroom cake.

The children come to us with so many root issues, causes, and deficiencies that's out of their control. How do we teach from year to year without shrinking in fear of knowing what we're going to face for 180 days? Simple, teachers have to V.O.W.

V.O.W. was a concept developed by yours truly, just like the "Window" perspective I talked about earlier. I needed something to help me stay focused on the goal of teaching and making a difference in the lives of my students. And now, I want to share this concept with you, a fellow educator.

So, again, how do you not sink in the fear of the basement confessionals of our students? Make a V.O.W. to reach the finish line and crossover into the winner's threshold. Let me explain.

There are nine points of impact for success I'd created to keep myself on target with new endeavors, I call it the V.O.W. 9 Points of Impact™. I even made a pictorial graphic as a demonstration.

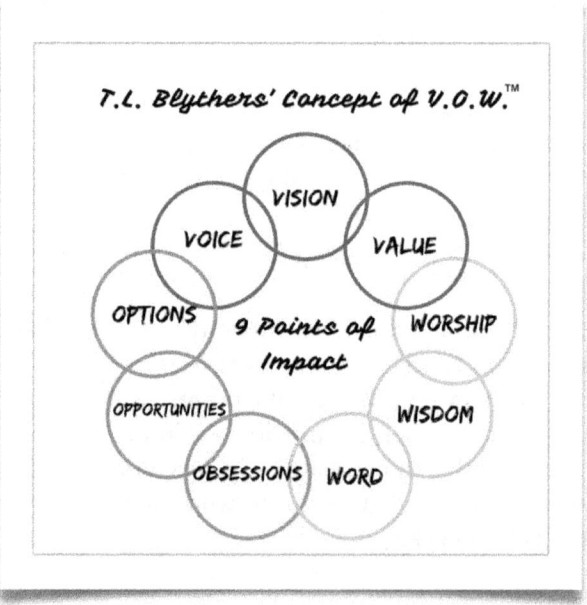

You see, there are some who think that success is going to track, attack, and Hocus Pocus—you will magically awake in the victor's circle. I wish it was that simple. Success takes strategic insight, planning, execution, and a lifetime of maintenance—which by the way is often forgotten, yet one of the most vital components to success.

During this "window of time" I have to chat with you, the goal is to paint a vivid image that will ignite your senses and purpose, while dulling the misguided perception that you can't make it or not being impactful. I'm also sharing this life-changing recipe in hopes that your goals, dreams, and visions intertwine simultaneously on a cataclysmic course that causes your mindset to be forever changed. Yes, it begins with the mind.

This whole notion about V.O.W. was birthed when I stepped out of the classroom to launch a consulting business and tour with my children's book, *Mika Dika Foster Kid*. I started thinking about a formula or "Life Cycle of Balance" and of course there's no perfect algorithm or unique design. It's all about how you incorporate it into your daily living.

The nine points of impact work together like nine circles interconnected. If one is out of sync, then your entire balance is compromised. Think of it as a type of system that regulates your life, just as the nervous, circulatory, digestive, and other human body systems work together. While serving time in the basement confessional as a servant leader, I heavily relied, and rely, on my oxygen tank, V.O.W. 9 Points of Impact™.

Vision, Voice, Value

We use our five senses for everything. Jesus performed miraculous healing like restoring sight to the blind. Obviously, there's priceless value in sight. Teachers provide sight to students who have been blinded by their life experiences, exposures, and traumas. We are the master creators of our students' life roadmaps.

Surely, some may think that Siri, software developed by Apple Incorporated, is the best auditory tool for global positioning. I disagree. It is the still small voice that we and students must follow that leads to a successful destination.

Who are you listening to? What are you watching? What are you digesting and ingesting? Protect the eyes and ear gates of your heart because what we absorb creates our perceptions. Then, we place a price and level of importance on that issue, person, or principality.

Where we are in life mentally and spiritually dictates and determines our value. Value your worth as a teacher while serving in the 'basement', and just because you're not seeing immediate changes doesn't mean you've failed. You plant the seeds in August and reap the harvest in May, so do not be discouraged.

The basement confessional creates reflective insight that requires every teacher to make necessary adjustments to their thoughts, beliefs, and actions. Within that nine-month window, there's voluntary, involuntary, uncontrollable, momentous growth for the student and teacher. A pregnancy can't be hidden for long. After nine months, "it's" going to be birthed.

Options, Opportunities, Obsessions

In the basement confessional, we are strategic apothecary creating positive circumstances and conditions that form better options for students. There is power in having choice and options.

Poverty is the oppressor and equalizer. Poverty of mindset is a future killer. It affects everything. It's not only money, but it's also about not having enough. Living in lack.

Students do not have enough faith, determination, self-esteem, love, self-pride, etc. Poverty is a huge factor while serving time in the basement confessional of students. We have to give them every opportunity to be successful. The root cause for many is failure. One success, just one win can catapult them to the next level. One thought, decision, action can revolutionize a family's lineage.

To be impactful, we have to be obsessed with their success. In education, test scores reign supreme. However, true success can and will always be measured far beyond test scores.

Word, Wisdom, Worship

Our livelihood is predicated on the belief system we've adopted. Reading, studying, and meditating on the word of God and other positive influences build personal growth and development.

Wisdom keeps us grounded and rooted while serving time in the basement confessional. Once the teacher is released from the basement confessional, we have to deal with the residue of "Even After".

Even after... the last paper has been graded, the last bus has trampled off-campus, the last soggy slice of pizza has been served, the last "all call" has been blasted over the intercom, we still wonder if they will make it home safely. Will they be able to sleep in peace? Are they being fed a healthy meal for dinner or are they waiting in Hell's Kitchen facing the fact that a meal is being withheld. We as teachers must apply wisdom especially during these moments of "even afters".

Lastly, Worship provides an outlet of peace. I am of the belief that an educator is a belief system engulfed with faith. The Word of God that stays upon the teacher's lip, in their heart, spirit, and eyesight is life-changing to a student's success. Worship plays a very important part in the lives of the educator. Your faith has something to ride up on. Your worship releases a sweet-smelling aroma to God. Think about how we gravitate to the aroma of homemade baked cookies, crispy bacon, freshly brewed coffee, and hot buttered popcorn. So is the sweet smelling aroma of true and authentic worship.

We live in the basement confessionals of our students' lives forever. There is no off switch until we retire, and then many return for a second term. While serving time, I've witnessed and heard about catastrophic, irreparable damage to students.

This is my confession. I cannot pinpoint a specific "worse" moment while in the basement confessional. Seeing a hungry kid hiding out to eat fruit and crackers behind my desk because an angry parent withheld grocery money doesn't compare to a student who's been traumatically abused and can no longer control their bodily functions. I cannot compare a child who's contracted a sexually transmitted disease due to rape to the one who has multiple personalities and hears voices. There's just no comparison.

Yet, in the midst of it all, there has been sobering and defining moments I've experienced in my career. The first one was when I received affirmations from prominent school officials defining my classroom as being like a spa. That was gratifying to know that I had created a positive, warm environment and was being honored as an effective, powerful, and relevant educator. Also satisfied that I was walking in the truth of the five-fold ministry of teaching that God graced upon me. The next revelatory moment was the realization that I had finally escaped the grisly grasp of poverty and now had an obligation to rescue others still drowning in the sea of hardship.

Finally at ground zero, I realized that because of poverty, there will always be casualties along the way, and this cold, crushing reality that some students do not want it bad enough and will be left behind in the basement.

So, what's my saving grace knowing all of this? How can I possibly go home to my seemingly nice, comfortable life with a warm, peaceful, safe bed and have a good night's sleep? This is how -- knowing that for nine months I made a conscious effort to give my best, I did what God called me to do, I treated every student fairly, treated every parent with dignity and respect. Most importantly, I chose to teach, equip, and empower to add value to students' lives.

The window is about to be closed and I will be released to the recovery room to rest and recuperate for 2-3 months. Oh yes, the recovery room... sometimes it can be just as daunting as the basement confessional. This room looks and takes on a different meaning for every educator. Time, silence, and peace is the perfect elixir to forget what should be forgotten about the 'basement confessional' experience.

Most educators, in general, take time and relax under the 'blanket of belief' knowing that God will refresh and reward. We rest our minds on the pillows of peace and patience, understanding that everything happens in HIS time.

Others self-medicate and meditate while licking and cleaning their wounds. Some seek professional therapy or find solace with family to cope with and rinse away the basement residue that causes a spirit of heaviness.

Imagine if you would, all teachers stepping out of the classroom simultaneously on the last day of school, taking off the white hazmat suit, and then enduring a painful scrub down.

Yet and still with hope, that spark that ignites expectation and the desire for an expected end. The unquenchable thirst for change, growth, and happiness is our driving force. We can be described as a resilient lotus, thriving in adversity, rising to the surface, unaffected and in full bloom.

"The Window" has closed. This is the truth, my realistic truth.

The Whole Truth & Nothing But the Truth, So Help Me Teachers!

Andrea Gibbs

Will I Ever Pass This Test?

What happens to a dream deferred? This is exactly how I felt as I struggled with employment as a teacher. You see, growing up I knew I would teach. I never once thought I would not be able to gain employment. I focused on completing my Bachelors of Science degree in Elementary Education, but never thought about being unemployed after obtaining my degree.

I was told education was my way out and that my degree was the answer, but I quickly learned that there were more questions and less answers.

I had already wasted so much time thinking when I graduate from high school that I would become a cosmetologist. I was married to my first husband before I finished high school, and we had an 11-month-old daughter. All I knew was that we had to make a living and provide for her. So, I went to Lawson State Cosmetologist school.

To be honest, cosmetology school was where I truly knew that teaching was my calling. I'll never forget my cosmetology instructor, Mrs. G, who changed my life. It was the way she delivered the lessons. She made me feel like cosmetology was a profession.

You see, I battled with choosing my career. Because I was so smart I don't think my family really wanted me to do hair. After all, my twin sister was in nursing school. I think they felt like doing hair was good for a side job, but that I should be doing something else. So, because Mrs. G knew the possibilities that the cosmetology industry would hold, I was confident and was able to stand proud in my decision.

God had already told me I would teach so I just coerced myself into thinking I would teach cosmetology. I'm so strong willed. I'll make a way into getting accomplished what I set out to do. I just didn't take into consideration that God's plan and will for me supersedes any plan I think I have.

Regardless, I had my life planned out that I would graduate at age 27, be remarried, and then be tenured at a school by the age of 30. I had it all figured out. All I had to do was graduate and everything else would fall in line (mind you I had a 9-year-old daughter now). I was separated from her dad at age 21, and now dating my current husband as I went to college. He took care of us financially so all I had to do was focus on school and being a mom.

My tenure through college was so easy. Classes were a breeze. I was top of the class, so I never really had to study. I'd taken test after test and aced them all. I mean, everything came easy for me. Well... until my junior year in college, the test of all tests for teachers: the Praxis! Let's just say God was preparing me, even back then.

The Praxis is a test that is administered by colleges for student entry into the teacher education program. The score determines whether an aspiring teacher can obtain their license to teach in a classroom environment.

So here it is, my junior year and time for me to take yet another test, but not just any test, the Praxis. Just as I had done with any other test, I went in the testing room confident and encouraged. I even prayed for everyone else as we went in ready to take the test.

Hours later, I really felt like I had accomplished something when I left. I left everything I had on that test, every knowledge, every dream, every experience... I gave it my all.

Other friends and students were nervous, but not me. I was assured of God's grace, mercy, and wisdom. After all, I prayed His Holy Spirit would help in areas where I fell short. Plus, I did my part by studying, right? I even hosted study parties led with prayer. Now, certainly God would answer with a resounding 'YES', right? Well that was the farthest thing from the truth.

As weeks that seemed like months went by, I checked the mail and there they were: My answer. The assurance I needed that God had called me to teach. After all, it was not only a criterion in order for me to teach one day, but it was Miles College criteria for graduation. You could not graduate without it.

So, as I opened the letter my heart felt like it would literally beat out of my chest. My hands became sweaty and I almost dropped the letter. I had to sit down. As my hands continued to shake, I finally got the letter opened and there it was in black, white and blue... Score needed to pass 136, your score 135.

Every ounce of color in me left, my heart began to ache, and I became so devastated. If you could fall into an instant depression, I'd say that's exactly what happened to me.

What am I supposed to do now? Certainly, this can't be right. So here we go back to the drawing board.

Ok I gave myself a few days to emotionally get over it and get a plan in place. Math was the area I scored the least, even though math was my favorite subject, so I decided to put my focus there. Plus, I had time, I wouldn't be a senior until next semester.

I studied, studied, and studied some more. Next time I take the Praxis I will surely pass it.

Fast forward, it's time again to take the test. The only thing I could think about was how it's almost time for the semester to end, and I really needed a passing score. My plan to student teach in August, graduate in May, and be employed by next school year was still in effect. I came up with this plan after high school when my first plan backfired.

So, it's test day (again), I'm calm and excited because I'm with my best friend and other friends who had been with me from the start of Miles College. We were in this thing together. We went in the testing room praying, trusting, knowing it was already done. Hours later, it was over and not so bad.

I went on and completed my college required classes -- all A's and one B. Summer was approaching and I had to sign up for student teaching (remember my plan to do this by August of the school year).

I was so nervous because I knew everyone else that I took the Praxis with had passed already. Seemed like it took me forever to get that letter opened. Here goes nothing. I opened the letter, and I felt my heart get heavy.

Lord this can't be right. My best friend standing on the side of me, I just handed her the paper. *Not again, Lord, 135 again one point away from passing again. How Lord? Why Lord?*

My best friend said, "No, Dre, not again!" She tried to comfort me, but it was nothing she could do.

How could you be happy for your best friend and everyone else who passed, but so disappointed for yourself? It was the hardest thing to ever do, but I had to pull from way down and be happy for them. I could have been more supportive though. That was a lesson all in itself. I did my very best but with age comes wisdom. I would have really pushed to be happier for their accomplishments and showed it more. But I was covered with disappointment.

So where do I go now? I could not graduate without passing this test. I went straight to the Praxis website to see when could I take the test again. I found the date, signed up, and paid the fee. Now I was on my own. No friends to study with, just me and God.

I truly talked to Him and shared all my fears and concern. *God, I know what I'm capable of, most importantly I know what You are capable of, so what's the deal God?*

I got closer to God than I had ever been. You see, I didn't want to lose my faith, I had to trust even though I couldn't trace. So, I took the test again. Mind you, the class I came with was about to graduate and they were student teaching. Meanwhile I was waiting on the test results to join them any day.

It was now February (months past the time in my original plan); and student teaching had been in session for about two weeks. I finally got my test scores: 141 Passed!!

Tears began to fall. I did it! Finally!!

I called my hubby first because he had to deal with the ugly side of me, the depressed me, the I don't want to go out in the world because everyone knew I failed my Praxis test me. I think he was more relieved than me (smile). I don't think he could have taken anymore. Then I called my mom and friends with the good news of finally passing the test.

After celebrating my win, I went up to Miles College to sign up for student teaching, only to be informed that I had to wait until August. There goes my plan. This new information meant that I wouldn't graduate until the year after I had planned. I was set back for a few months, but after I thought about it, I decided it was probably best.

I had a whole wedding planned for that year prior to student teaching anyway. Sometimes separation is good. You must learn that your path is not the same as someone else's path. God was teaching me to stand alone. I also became frustrated with my school.

Now don't get me wrong, I had the very best instructors anyone could have asked for. The staff at Miles College Education Department was awesome. I felt like maybe perhaps I had not been prepared efficiently to take the test. Maybe a little ill-guided. We waited to take the Praxis when I was almost a senior in college, I had taken Math and English in my earlier college years, so long ago but that's basically what the test was centered around.

I thought that the test would be based off what I had learned through my education classes, how to teach more so than what to teach. That was not the case. So really there was no reason to wait until it was almost time to graduate college. My Praxis test had less to do with pedagogy skills, but more what I knew academically. So why was I told by the school to wait? That really frustrated me after all I had gone through to finally pass. And I knew students who took ten times to pass the test! It was very discouraging. I remember having to encourage many people to keep on pushing in spite of that small obstacle. It could have been enough for any of us to quit.

The Whole Truth & Nothing But the Truth, So Help Me Teachers!

I remember that also was the year Miles College implemented the Child Development Program. It was for those people who wanted to do more of a daycare, pre-school, or pre-k program. I heard someone say that it was for those who couldn't pass the Praxis but still wanted the opportunity to graduate. Some of my friends chose the dual degree route where they would obtain a degree in Child Development, then turned around and pass the Praxis for that degree too. Whichever path we decided to follow, the main thing was that we didn't give up. We endured to the end.

Getting back to the story... It's now time for me to student teach. You heard me say this several times already, but I didn't tell you what that was. Well, student teaching is an internship for prospective teachers. Before we can get our license to teach in a classroom, while we are still in college, we have to complete an internship in a licensed teacher's classroom.

A school's administrator would select one of their teachers that they felt had exemplary pedagogy skills to pour all of themselves into student teachers. These exemplary teachers, also called cooperating teachers, would monitor the prospective teachers and give them feedback. That was a huge responsibility. They were giving up their students for months to student teachers. Consequently, the prospective teachers had to do lesson plans, grade papers, check roll, teach lessons, have classroom management... the whole nine yards.

Anyone who knew me knew that I loved teaching upper elementary grade. At that point my daughter was 11-years-old, so I was used to bigger children. When Mrs. H, my cooperating teacher, said I needed to do half the semester in kindergarten and the other half in fifth grade, I began to panic.

Now that was scary. *Lord, how am I going to make it through?*

The first day of kindergarten I got my schedule and saw that I would be in there from August to October. *Lord, help me make it through* (smile). I mean, my degree would be in Elementary, not Early Childhood Education.

I remember kindergarteners being all over the place running and jumping around, and just learning alphabets and sounds. Now here we go! Day one was an eye opener. I thought teaching kindergarten would be more of a structured script: What letter is this, now what sound does it make... but I learned quickly from Mrs. H that in kindergarten you actually teach. I was in Heaven!

I taught like I would teach a third grader, just in a way that a kindergartener could understand. I made it fun and I was amazed at how much and well they learned. I remember some letters the parents wrote and I was so thankful that Mrs. H shared the notes with me. Parents would say things like 'homework was a breeze' and 'I didn't have to help with Math' and 'my child knew exactly what to do'. That was the highlight of my experience and one I would never forget.

October flew by and on to teach the fifth graders. Now that was where I was the most comfortable. My cooperating teacher, Mrs. K, was awesome. The curriculum was a little more rigorous. Learning what all it took to be an effective teacher was exhausting. I learned that we had to deal with way more than just academics. Some of the children in that particular district had real issues that they dealt with on an everyday basis.

Stuff that was so bad that I don't see how they had the time or energy to try and learn anything. It taught me that their time was valuable and when I taught, I had to be interesting and purposeful. I had to make sure that the time I was given to make a difference in their lives was impactful. So I made up my mind that I would teach every single chance I got, while building relationships with them.

I learned some children didn't eat over the weekend, and so some teachers would keep food in their closets so the children wouldn't have to think about food when they were at school. I learned quickly that I would have to be a counselor, doctor, friend, parent, sometimes preacher, whatever the child needed at that time. And all of that was before I began to teach one single word!

I knew at that moment that it was going to take some hard work and dedication, but I was up for it. I was ready for every challenge teaching would bring. As December approached, and I was finishing up my last presentation, I reflected on the decision I made to become a teacher. I just wanted to make a difference in the world. I just wanted to help children.

My mom home schooled me and my twin sister, and she was also a Sunday school teacher. You see, teaching was in my blood. I began teaching children's church and Sunday school too. At that time I met the Pastor's wife at our church, and she was the kind of teacher that made me fall in love with teaching on another level. First Lady (what I called the Pastor's wife) had a thing for words. To hear her speak, she would captivate her audience. She would take you on a ride. You would get lost in a story. So, as I would listen to her interact with the Sunday school students, I realized my calling was deeper.

First Lady grabbed a hold of me and said, "I need you." And I knew exactly what she meant. She was talking about teaching God's Word to His people. I told you that my calling was much deeper than the classroom I taught in.

The Word of God was something my mom taught me as a child. She would sit me down at the kitchen table with a dictionary, concordance, and a reference Bible. My mom was a very intelligent woman, but she taught me to look up meanings to words I didn't know. She wouldn't just tell me the meaning, she made me look it up myself.

So, we studied the Bible. Now, of course the Holy Spirit was how we really learned the scripture meaning, but we used other resources to guide our understanding. Certainly, that was God's purpose. The Word of God was in me now I could help get it out.

As I began my career as a teacher, I also began my calling as a teacher of God's Word. Though I knew my career in teaching would ultimately be the catalyst of my financial stability, I found teaching God's Word to be more fulfilling.

I still get goosebumps to this day when I teach God's Word. Every now and then I have those goosebumps teaching in the classroom, but it is something about God's Word.

So, as I readied to walk across the stage to graduate, I was excited about where my life was headed. I was ready to begin my career teaching and I was also excited about learning more about God's Word while teaching His children... whether in the classroom or the church room.

I knew that teaching was a calling and a gift, and I approached each opportunity as an assignment. On to the next phase of my assignment. Now I had the opportunity to go out into the real world and implement the things I learned during my matriculation through Miles College, my student teaching experience, and life experiences.

The Whole Truth & Nothing But the Truth, So Help Me Teachers!

PART TWO: LESSONS LEARNED

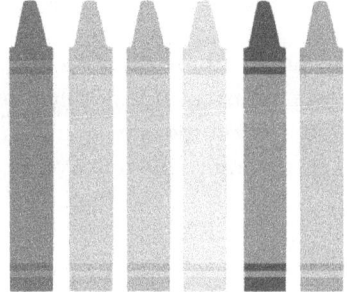

The Whole Truth & Nothing But the Truth, So Help Me Teachers!

Vicki Kirk May

They Are Out To Kill Me!

Okay is it just me or do you think there's a target on your back? I promise you there were seasons in my educational career when I thought they were out to kill me. I'm going to keep it at "they" because "they" is so much more provocative. Besides, everybody's "they" is different.

They come to steal your thunder when you do a great job on a lesson or pull off a difficult task. They come when you teach with integrity and decide you are not going to give the star football player a passing grade when he is failing. They really show up when you decide to do your job and not complain when everyone else around is singing the blues. They come to suck the very air you breathe out of you. They want you damaged. They want you broken. They want you dead!

So maybe not literally dead, but they want your dreams and goals of making a difference in the lives of children to die. They know if your dreams die, so do you and all the children assigned to you. So what do they do? They devise a plan of attack. It is systematic, schematic, and surreptitious.

How do you fight against them when you don't know they exist, you don't know when they are coming, or what they are really after? My prayer is that as I share my story, some of it, if not all of it, will resonate with you. Hopefully, you will feel compelled to take the action steps to avoid what is out to kill your passion to educate.

At one point in my career I really felt unfulfilled because I confined my passion for education and helping others to the four walls of my classroom. However, after many years of being frustrated and very uncomfortable in my calling to teach, I began to step outside the classroom, move beyond the school, and effectuate change in different ways.

With freedom comes the fight. I thought that everything would be peaches and cream. Finally I was happy. I was living in passion and walking in my purpose. I went into my classroom ready and willing to make a difference one student, one teacher, one parent at a time. It would be smooth sailing right? That would be a negative.

Even though I was fulfilling my purpose on the earth, that didn't excuse me from experiencing attacks. Just in case you don't know, the moment you decide to really get serious about being a great educator and playing full out is the moment the fight begins. They are coming for you so be ready! They are passion killers.

Passion killers come to stop you from moving forward, keep you stuck in mediocrity, destroy your self-esteem, and render you hopeless and helpless so that you die having not fulfilled your life's purpose.

I believe that we answer the call to educate by taking what God has given us... the things that we are passionate about and serving our community locally and globally. I believe that it is not as hard as people make it. The very thing that we love to do can change the world if we allow it. I believe that your personality, passion, and purpose when connected properly activates the power that is in us. It is that power that we must use to effectuate change, in ourselves, our families, in our students, our parents, our communities, and in the world.

However, as educators, we cannot serve our students, let alone the world, if we do not walk in our purpose. We must prepare ourselves to deal with whatever comes our way that tries to kill, steal, and destroy our God-given visions and dreams concerning our call to teach. I wish I could tell you that it is going to be smooth and easy, but the truth is your acceptance of the call comes with some heat. Turbulence, uneasiness, separation, isolation, and much more joins you as you walk in your purpose.

Teaching is hard and there is no need for me to sugar coat. Even on my best days when I go home and share with my husband how well everything went in the classroom that day doesn't negate the fact that it was just as hard as it was good. Therefore, because it is already difficult, we don't need anything else keeping us from doing what we are supposed to do.

So what do I mean? Sometimes we can be our own worst enemy when we are walking in our purpose. Sometimes forces are working against us so we can't be the world changers we're destined to be.

In my 20 years of teaching, there were passion killers that attacked me at certain times in my career. They attacked after every success and accomplishment. They attacked whenever unity was at its strongest. So as I share my lessons learned with you, I pray you can avoid the passion killers that come to stop you from being the difference in the lives of the children you have been assigned. Let me explain these passion killers and how I was able to fight back against them.

Passion Killer #1: Stinkin' Thinkin'

> *Stinkin' Thinkin' is a thought pattern that encourages, fosters, and nurtures a negative inner voice that speaks gloom and doom all the time.*

This passion killer destroys your self-esteem. It devalues you, beats you up and leaves your dreams for dead. It reminds you of your past failures. It picks at you first thing in the morning when you look in the mirror.

It says things like, "My hair is nappy!", "My face too fat! I'm too fat!", "Look at my body, it is horrible".

When you walk in the classroom, it says things like, "My room isn't a nice as others", "I am not as creative as Miss S down the hall".

Stinkin' Thinkin' is a powerful passion killer because it's not the thoughts or words of outside interferences. It's what you say about yourself to yourself. If you can identify with this passion killer, and it is keeping you from being the committed educator, then take these action steps.

1. Command your morning before you go to bed. At bedtime, take about five minutes and speak to the upcoming day. Tell it how it's going to go. For example, I would say at bedtime, "Tomorrow I will stay positive, I will not focus on anything negative. Everything I am believing God for will happen. I matter and what I do matters." I would speak with clarity, compassion, and confidence. Other things I would say at bedtime, "I have money I know not of. Love, peace, and joy greets me everyday."
2. Before you get out of bed every morning, say something good about yourself and re-iterate what you said the night before.
3. Write as many life-draining words as you can think of that you say to yourself, and then write down the opposite of that

which are life-giving words. For example, one of my life draining words were, "There's no need in me trying this strategy, the kids won't use it". Next to that statement, I would write, "My students are eager and ready to learn. Learning happens in my classroom" and "I have all the resources I need to serve my students". Once you turn your life-draining words into life-giving words, write them (the life-giving words) on sticky notes and place them on the mirror in the bathroom, on the refrigerator door, in your office or cubicle at work, in the closet in your classroom, or on the wall by your desk. Place these life-giving words sticky notes anywhere you frequent.

You are transferring negative energy to positive energy, therefore there is a transference of power. By placing the affirmations (life-giving words) in areas where you will see them, it will cause you to focus more on being positive.

Additionally, you are creating your world. How cool is that?! You are telling the universe what you expect and it has to line up with your words because it knows you have dominion. Remember, you are giving the universe a different assignment. It always did what you said, this time your words are creating a better world for you and your students.

Passion Killer #2: Being Unclear

It is difficult to complete your goals if you are unclear about who you are or what you want. Being sure of who you are as a man or woman first is vitally important when you are trying to reach your goals. It is important to know what your likes and dislikes are, what makes you happy, what makes you sad, what excites you, what motivates you, what stops you dead in your tracks.

The truth is most of us don't take time to find out who we really are. We rely on the perceptions of others or we become satisfied with surface knowledge because to go deep into who you really are can be very painful. In order to accomplish your dreams and live a life of passion and purpose, you must be willing to get to know who you are and accept yourself -- flaws and all.

The truth of the matter is, on the journey to knowing you, it is going to get real dark and gloomy. You're going to realize that there is a lot about yourself that you don't like. You are going to remember the times you were hurt, disappointed, misused, abused, cheated on, and lied to. You are going to remember all the times that you were unfair, that you lied, cheated, talked about folks. You're going to remember the times that you weren't a good parent, spouse, coworker, and educator. You are going to remember what it felt like to be molested and raped. You are going to remember all the negative words that were told to you. AND THEN YOU ARE GOING TO HURT AND HURT BAD.

But this time you are going to allow yourself a moment to feel the hurt, deal with it, and put it where it belongs... in the past.

Teaching is so very important. A great teacher frames the world. Therefore the world needs teachers who know who they are and how they are supposed to show up in the world. These are some action steps you can take if you want to get to know yourself better.

1. *Revisit your past.* Allow yourself to see the worst in you and the best in you, and write down the lesson you have learned. You will realize how great you are and that everything that happened to you made you into the awesome person you are today. There will also be an awareness that your 'down time' was your 'development time'.

2. *Date yourself.* Go to the movies and dinner by yourself. Get to know what you really like and don't like. You will fall in love with yourself--the good, the bad, and the ugly.

3. *Develop non-negotiables for yourself in every area of your life and write them down.* It will help you to create safe and healthy boundaries for your life. It will also serve as an alert when

you see yourself giving in to what you have already said NO to.

Passion Killer #3: Fear

Fear paralyzes you and keeps you stuck. Fear tethers you to the familiar, the comfortable, to average and mediocrity. Fear is created in your brain. It is a protection mechanism that keeps you from negative consequences. Fear requires the idea of something bad happening to you.

Our meaning determines our experience in the universe. Most of us do not correctly identify what we are afraid of. We identify the wrong target. For example, some people, and I was one of them, would say that they are afraid of flying. No one really has a fear of flying, you have a fear of dying in a plane crash. You don't have a fear of heights, you have a fear of falling. You see the difference? Identifying the fear is key to stopping it from interfering with you realizing your dreams.

Now there are three big fears that you have to get rid of if you are to reach your goals: fear of failure, fear of rejection, and fear of success. Additionally, here are a few facts about fear itself:

1. Fear doesn't come alone. It brings anxiety, depression, illness, discouragement etc.
2. Fear makes you judgmental.
3. Fear can rob you of your health.
4. Fear will keep you from asking for help.
5. Fear will make you buy into 'quick fixes'.
6. Fear will bleed over into other areas of your life.
7. Fear is the most deadliest thing in our bodies.

So how do you fight against this passion killer? You take action. You jump!! Jump knowing that you are fully loaded. You don't have to wait for understanding, perfect it along the way. Just jump! If you jump, you won't have time to be afraid.

Passion Killer #4: Un-forgiveness

Un-forgiveness is a passion killer because it hinders your success in all areas of your life. When un-forgiveness resides in your heart, it is like taking a poisonous pill of resentment, bitterness, and revenge. It is hard to prosper when your body is filled with poison.

To be consumed by un-forgiveness can kill you slowly over time. It literally steals your happiness and ultimately your life. The one that hurts you the most is the one you seem unable to forgive: YOU. We remain stuck in our current situation because we can't defeat our worst enemy: Self.

In order to move past the hurt and pain of the past, we must forgive. Forgiveness leads to self-love and acceptance. Soon you will find yourself being compassionate towards others, even the ones who hurt you. Before you know it, the weight of un-forgiveness no longer holds you down. Forgiveness releases freedom to live out your best life.

Here are some actions you can take to help you release un-forgiveness:

1. *Say to yourself: I forgive you for (fill in the blank).* At this point you are releasing yourself of every bad decision, every self-inflicted emotional wound, and guilt. It causes you to move forward and to be forgiving to others.

2. *Say to the one you are forgiving: I forgive you for (fill in the blank; be specific and say the offense, but don't blame or re-hash what the person has done).* If the person you need to forgive is not living you may want to have someone you trust to stand in that person's place so that you can say what needs to be said.

Passion Killer #5: Negative Words

You may have heard someone say this before to be careful of what goes into your ear gates. There is a reason for this warning. Most of you know that what you listen to affect you either negatively or positively. Conversations take place to persuade, inform, or entertain you. No matter what the purpose of the conversation or dialogue, a response comes afterwards through our thoughts and/or actions.

Our brain is pretty powerful and we are constantly thinking. Consequently, about 60,000 of those thoughts are negative thoughts that, if you are not careful, can turn into negative words. Negative words grow and take root. Negative conversations are contagious. You will not reach your goals talking about other people. That is a fact.

So here's how you fight against negative words:

1. When people start talking negative in your presence, be the example and dismiss yourself. Easy as that! Remove yourself from the conversation. Don't answer their calls, etc. Protect your space. Protect your ear gates.

2. If you are unable to remove yourself physically from a negative conversation, then put a positive spin on whatever the person is saying. It keeps your mind on positive things so that you can reach your goals.

The truth and the whole truth is this: don't let the noise of life keep you from hearing your true calling as a teacher, as an educator, living with passion and walking in your purpose. The noise, also known as passion killers, can come to you in the form of bill collectors, family members, responsibilities and more. Take time to connect, reconnect, and resurrect your passion and purpose again.

Dr. Marquita Blades

It's Okay To Teach Who You Love

Teachers are supposed to love their students. All of them.

Teachers are expected to see all students as the same regardless of what they look like, where they come from, or how they behave. All of them.

Teachers are not supposed to like one group of students more than others. But they do. Most of them will not tell you this, but, teachers do not like all students.

In fact, there are certain types of students that they do not like, do not care to work with, and should avoid at all costs.

I am at a point now where I am not only able to see this, but admit it as well. I used to believe that I loved all students, but as my career wore on, I realized that there are some students who I absolutely do not care to work with.

The whole truth is that certain types of students, who come from certain types of homes, exhibit certain types of behaviors. PERIOD.

A good teacher can spot these students a mile away and are almost never wrong when we pre-assess these students. This fact in and of itself is neither good or bad. It simply is.

I once worked at an all-girls charter school and I thought that working in that setting was what I was supposed to do because of my own background. I felt as if I owed these young brown girls the same inspiration that my teachers had given me. I'd left a school that I loved, kids that I loved, and a position teaching the subject that I loved, because I felt an obligation to my demographic. It didn't hurt that the administration also made it sound like an incredible opportunity for growth (insert extended eye roll).

Shortly after accepting this new position, I found that it was not for me. The students were not at all what I was accustomed to. Yes, they were young black girls, but I had nothing in common with them. There was no chemistry. No matter what I did, I was not able to connect with these students or the mission of the school.

My personal belief system did not align with the mission of the school or how they dealt with students and parents. For these reasons, I resented the school and everything in it – from the administration all the way down to the students!

Teachers are made to feel guilty about having preferences. I'm sorry to say this, but all students are not created equal, nor are all teachers. This does not mean that they deserve any less, but it does impact who should be working with them.

Think about it. It is perfectly okay for a student and/or their parents to object to having a certain type of teacher. It is okay for students to have preferences, although the teacher may not have done anything to the student personally. Some students just don't like and won't learn from certain teachers. Why is it not okay for teachers to object to the type of students who enter their classrooms?

Just as there are different types of tools to be used for various purposes, there are several types of teachers who should be working with different types of students. While it may be a teacher's intention to work with and help all students, the fact is that not all teachers are good for all students. Teachers just don't want to admit it though.

Here's what I know about me: behavior management is not my thing. I'm just not good at discipline. I don't like to tell students to do something multiple times.

I do not understand how people are not able to control themselves. It is a concept that I simply cannot relate to. This is due to my own upbringing. I was raised that certain behaviors are only appropriate for certain situations, and that it is up to the individual, regardless of age, to make that determination. No one had to tell me to control myself, so it irritated me to have to tell others to control themselves.

I taught high school, so based on my beliefs and experiences, I had an expectation that high school-aged students should be able to decide which behaviors were appropriate in a classroom and which ones were not. Several high school students were either unable or mostly, unwilling, to make these decisions about their behaviors. Those were, and are not my ideal students. I like students who know how to conduct themselves without being told.

I am an instruction kind of teacher. I thrive in the lesson planning department. I have a talent and passion for creating engaging and innovative lessons. Students typically enjoy my class, even if they don't like the subject – biology, chemistry, and physics. I just have a way of making it fun and interesting for any student who wants to do well.

Having to teach students who lack self-control meant that I had to use the energy that would have been reserved for instruction to manage behaviors. Rather than focusing on what I am naturally good at and what benefits students, I had to spend many days doing that for which I have no talent or passion: behavior management.

In any other industry, you would not expect a person to work in a department outside of his or her expertise, but such is the case with teaching. It is rare that you find building administrators who strategically hire teachers based on what they like and are good at. Most administrators hire based on need, availability, and sometimes certification.

On the flip side, some teachers enjoy the challenge of molding a difficult student into shape. I admire those teachers. I just know that I am not one of them.

Many teachers are inspired by students who need additional support and mentoring. Working with these types of students comes naturally for them. While it is acceptable by society for a teacher to say, "I want to work with at-risk students", it is not acceptable for others to say, "I only want to work with high-achieving students".

Every cup of tea has its saucer!

Teachers are expected to sacrifice themselves and their own happiness for the benefit of the students. This is a notion that I simply do not agree with.

How can an unhappy teacher be effective with students? Students absorb the energy that is radiated by teachers. When teachers are not excited about the work, students suffer. We should want teachers to be excited about the work. We should want them to be excited to see their students each day.

Realtors have the luxury of only working with high-end clients if that's what they prefer. Teachers are shamed for making this designation.

In all fairness, teachers bear a lot of the responsibility in this phenomenon. No one forces a teacher to work in any school. Teachers can choose not to work in certain types of environments with certain types of students; but many feel that they have to go where the jobs are.

Obviously, the jobs in more desirable schools will fill quicker than those at less desirable schools. This trend is evident that a lot of teachers really do prefer to work with students who come to school prepared to learn. These positions, once filled, rarely open up unless someone moves out of state or retires.

The next person in line is usually one who is a member of an exclusive short list of candidates, making it nearly impossible for some teachers to even have a chance at landing one of these jobs.

In the less desirable schools, classes for high-achievers are few and far between, so once a teacher gets that course load, any other teacher expecting to teach those courses can usually forget about it.

Because teachers are committed to the work, they would rather teach anywhere, even if it does not align with their core values, beliefs, and personal preferences. That is how I felt for a long time.

For some teachers, especially those who are first-generation college graduates, we feel obligated to teach in the less desirable schools knowing that other teachers are not interested. We – literally we, because I am a first generation college grad – tell ourselves that we must accept the charge of educating those from similar backgrounds as ourselves. It is our responsibility!

No matter how tough it is, we will do it! Don't get me wrong. It is the honorable thing to do and we all owe it to the communities that we come from to give something back; however, some of us are not built to teach in the neighborhoods that we come from. It's just not in us! Well, it wasn't in me.

After honest reflection on my career, I came to the conclusion that I was most effective and happy as a teacher when I taught students who did not share my same background. Students who come from the same type of environment as I had actually found little to no value in the experiences and wisdom I attempted to share with them.

In their eyes, I was not "hood enough", talked "like a white lady", and was "too put together".

I often "did too much" and had expectations that were too high. I spent so much time trying to reach those students when they had decided they did not want to learn from me. In return, I was often frustrated and hated going to work.

In my eyes, those students were excuse makers who were facing the same situation that many people before them had already overcome. To me, they just didn't want to get it together. If they wanted to do better, they could; they just needed to change their mindset.

Do you see how this can be problematic? A teacher is supposed to feel compassion for students in tough situations. In many cases, I did not. I felt as if I had overcome my hardships, they could and should work hard to do the same, especially if they had a passionate teacher who was dedicated to their academic success.

I finally came to the conclusion that, for me, mindset is more important than background. I was happiest when I taught students who were confident in their abilities and always did their best. I could see the fruits of my labor on a daily basis. I felt as if the work I was doing was making a difference. I could actually see the difference.

I enjoyed working with kids who were optimistic about their futures and who found value in the personal stories that I shared with them, as opposed to those who only chose to complain and misbehave each day.

That's not to say that these students did not have problems. Many of them did, but their mindsets were not that of defeat. These students knew that if they put in the work, they'd be able to overcome their obstacles.

I am most effective when I work with students who think this way. I am able to do so much more with them. When introducing them to new concepts, rather than immediately saying, "that's hard", they'd perk up and say, "let me try".

Just think how much better instruction would be if teachers could teach the students they love!

What if teachers did not take certain positions out of scarcity or obligation, and held out for the position and environment they truly desired?

Students are better off when their teachers are happy, healthy, and inspired. Far too many teachers are remaining in toxic, dangerous, unproductive school environments for far too long working with students that they don't love.

Far too many teachers give up on the populations they serve and refuse to provide instruction to the best of their abilities because they know the students will not live up to their expectations.

Can you say *worksheet teacher*? You know the ones we accuse of simply collecting a paycheck. Do you think that would happen if the teacher were in an environment where they could use their true gifts and talents with students who appreciated them?

What would happen if the teachers who loved to motivate, encourage, and inspire took their places with the students who needed that most? It has to become okay for teachers to work with the students they love.

Education is the only profession that discourages self-care and self-preservation. Teachers are made to believe that they are bad people if they want to work in an environment that makes them happy. Teachers are led to believe that it is selfish to want to work in the highest paid districts. Teachers are led to believe that if they are teaching Honors or Advanced Placement courses, they have taken the easy way out.

It's no wonder teachers get burned out and become ineffective. We are taught and made to believe that we really don't matter!

We have to have enough belief in ourselves and our abilities to know that we don't have to suffer in an unhealthy work environment and if we can't find one that suits us, perhaps we should not teach for that term!

The Whole Truth & Nothing But the Truth, So Help Me Teachers!

Nicole Brown-Horston

I Am Somebody

Over the course of my 20+ years as a facilitator of learning, I have so many real accounts of the psychological and emotional effects we as educators have on children. Each of these experiences has touched and transformed my life in such a way that I have made it my life's mission to go above and beyond to connect with each child I service.

While I have always known the importance of affirming a child, I believe that this particular lesson hit home in the worst way when my son began having difficulty learning in middle school. My son had always loved learning, but I can remember he started coming home with such a negative notion of school during his seventh-grade year. As a parent and an educator who taught seventh grade, I couldn't put my finger on what brought about this change. The guilty conscience I felt when the students I was teaching were excelling and my child was not, I knew I had to take action and quickly.

For those of you who may not be aware of the research on middle schoolers, it indicates that success in middle school is a central indicator of whether a student will drop out of high school. From seventh grade onward, students are no longer given as much hand-holding and coddling as they were given in earlier years. They are asked to be more accountable and responsible for their learning, actions, and behavior. During seventh grade, students also become bombarded with many social changes that impact their success in school, and they are expected to suddenly become equipped with the tools to deal with such changes. Sometimes, without any support.

After doing my own research into what was taking place in my son's classes, I found that many of his teachers' approaches to learning were a lot different from mine, especially when it came to building personal relationships and encouraging an environment that was conducive to learning.

As I sat in some of his classes, I saw many of the teachers lacked the same discipline that they required of their students. Even when my son would explain to me the harsh words that were used when certain students asked for help, the lack of classroom management, and how some teachers would be doing other things during class time instead of teaching (on their cell phones, reading the newspaper, working on Graduate coursework, etc.), I didn't believe him. Until I observed these issues first-hand.

Of course, this put me in an awkward space because on one account these were my colleagues I was evaluating. On the other hand, I knew I had to do what was in the best interest of my son. Rather than report them to their superiors, I chose to build up my son's self-esteem so that he would be prepared to deal with these situations mentally. That was when I introduced him to Affirmation Therapy.

Positive affirmations are a popular technique used in Cognitive Behavioral Therapy to replace existing thoughts that may be untrue and hurtful. It also helped to manifest the change that I desired for my son as well as what he wanted to accomplish.

While I knew that I couldn't change the effects of what his teachers did to him in the past, I was determined to change his mindset moving forward. Each day, I would recite different affirmations with him before I went away for work, and he went to school. Below is the one that I wrote specifically for my son, and it has also been used in my classroom year after year.

> I am Somebody: I am somebody. I am capable, loving and teachable. Therefore, I can learn. I will respect myself and others. I will not waste time because time is too precious, and I am too bright. I am somebody.

Affirming children into believing that they can become anyone they set their desires may have its challenges, but it's worth it. Think of it in reference to a beautifully wrapped present. You have to peel away at all the wrappings to see the real gift that's inside. The same applies to children. You have to be ready to discover their abilities as you peel away the layers.

A perfect example of this would be a child's behavior or classroom antics. Most feel that this behavior will result in failure. These students are the ones who will be kicked out of the classroom or even school the most, and labeled incorrigible. On the contrary, I have found that a student who exhibits disruptive behavior is seeking to be understood. As such, as the professional, you must accept the challenge to help uncover their true gifts.

Teachers must have the patience, diligence, and consistency to help the child realize their full potential. I know this can be a hearty feat with over thirty kids in a classroom, state and federal mandates, and a school district imposing unrealistic demands but we must try.

Each day, parents or guardians entrust seven hours to someone who may not always share their philosophy on how to reach their child. As a parent or guardian, it is ultimately up to you to impart your expectations. And no matter what happens in the classroom, you must understand the power your child has within to succeed, and you must be your child's advocate.

It is my consistent belief that:

1. You must be an active participant in your child's life. Don't solely rely on the school system to educate, empower, or to elevate your child.

2. You must never give up on your child. Even when your child doesn't perform as they should, go above and beyond to figure out the source of the undesirable behavior. Don't always blame your child because there could be an underlying reason.

3. Finally, you must not fail your child by permitting others to degrade or demean them, even if they are a professional. You must teach your child how to use their voice to speak up about issues they may have in the classroom. Then, follow the chain of command in order to resolve them.

The techniques that I described above brought about a positive change in my own son's life. Today, he is a productive member of society who is helping young people to succeed. He is a testament to how positive affirmations can be a powerful tool to help you change your mood, your state of mind, and your outlook on life.

I pride myself on the fact that I am a parent and a facilitator of learning. It is up to me to make the learning experience of each child I encounter easier. I must assist, guide, supervise and redirect each of them to their expected outcome.

Is the task sometimes arduous and the journey sometimes uncertain? Most definitely! But I'm up for the challenge.

The Whole Truth & Nothing But the Truth, So Help Me Teachers!

Andrea Gibbs

Will I Ever Get a Job?

Now that my internship, also known as student teaching, was complete and I now hold a Bachelor's of Science degree in Elementary Education, Summa Cum Laude, I was ready for my new career! But no one told me that there was a shortage of teaching jobs in 2010. I assumed you obtained a degree then you walked in and got your job.

During the last few months of my student teaching internship, I guess my new husband and I celebrated a little too much, and I soon found out that my now 7-year-old prince and genius was on the way. I walked across the stage seven months pregnant. I graduated May 2010 and our son was born July 2010.

I never will forget that I was so excited he was coming but, most importantly, he would be a summer baby. So, in my mind I still had time to spend with him and to join the workforce in a few weeks when school started in August.

I began to send resumes through email, dropped them off at schools, called friends who were employed, called my old professors, anything I thought that would help. Week after week, nothing. I learned quickly that it was who you know.

As I went from school to school, both private and public, I started to wonder if I would ever get a job. It was something about the school secretaries. I wondered if my resumes ever reached the principals. I had run into a few secretaries where I felt like I did not want to work at that school anyway. They had some of the worst attitudes I had ever seen! I thought, 'Oh Lord and they are around children and parents every day?'

I remember this one secretary that stuck out from the rest. I stood in that office what had to have been at least 25-30 minutes before she even acknowledged my presence. She looked at me several times but never said one word. What bothered me the most about that encounter was that she had no idea who I was. I could have been from the State department, local board or district, most importantly a concerned parent. I was so upset.

Looking back almost ten years later, I am glad I never got a call back. They could have made my teaching experiences bad.

As August came and went, I was discouraged. I thought, 'Ok, I have a newborn, my husband is working and doing well so I'll just enjoy this bundle of joy until something happens.'

I just knew it would be soon. After all, I was highly qualified and certified so I was sure the State would call me. I continued to submit resumes online to schools. Month after month I waited until a whole year passed and still no job.

This continued for years. After the third year, I really began to pray. I told God I had trusted Him all of my life, and He promised me that He would take care of me and my family.

Around that time, Hubby came to me and said that he wanted to change careers to become a police officer.

"Well, ok if that's what you want to do," I responded.

Actually, it did not sound like a bad idea. He took the written test and passed. Later took the physical agility part and passed that as well. So then he was accepted to the police academy.

You would think that was something to celebrate, right? Ok sure, but we learned real quick that we would be taking a severe pay cut. So, mind you he was the bread winner and, though I had a degree, I could not get a teaching job no matter how hard I tried.

I went back to God. I mean obviously He did not hear me the first time. After prayer, we decided that we were going to trust God; and so my hubby joined the police academy.

In the meantime, I decided to return to school for my Master's degree. I figured I could enroll in some online courses. Maybe with more education and degrees under my belt that would give me a better opportunity at getting a job.

After a year and a half more without a job or even a call back, I quit school! I was seven classes shy of my Masters. I was discouraged and started thinking that maybe teaching must not be for me.

My unemployment was causing a financial strain on my marriage. I needed to work so I started to substitute teach. Finally, a teacher was retiring in the middle of the school year and I was called in as a permanent sub.

You see, the whole time I was putting in applications, no one ever called for an interview. I kept saying to myself that if they just met me they would love me. They would see how much I really loved children and wanted to teach. I would do my very best and they would not regret hiring me. Words I never got a chance to say because I was never given the opportunity to meet them face-to-face.

As I loaded my application on the State Department website, I often wondered if they liked me until they saw that I only had experience in student teaching. Was that the reason they skipped me? Was that the reason they never called back for an interview? How could I get experience without a job?

I was a substitute teacher until the end of the school year and was a great candidate to receive the position permanent. Then the system did a split and moved the sixth graders to the middle school. The principal had to place all tenured teachers, and the new and non-tenured teachers were left out. That was heart breaking for me. I waited patiently but faithfully for months for a call back that never came.

What would I do? I went back to substituting. Hubby and I had been married for about five years and our son was four years old. Even though I home schooled him, I knew the importance of social skills so I decided he should go to Pre-K. That was the best decision I made and the catalyst for my future employment.

So I sign him up and he was accepted. I volunteered almost every day. I mean, if they were having something at the school, I was there. I was there so much that they found out I had a teaching degree. They sent me to headquarters and I became the Lead Teacher at my son's school. It was the best years of my life. I could finally do what I had been called to do... touch lives and teach.

My students' parents were everything. They would bring their children in and sign-in everyday, then pick them up at the end of the school day. So, we bonded. That relationship building was something I think public schools should adopt worldwide.

Matter of fact, I still follow my students' progress today and I will proudly say that 80-85% of them are all honor roll students. The relationship I built with their parents remain in tact as well.

Okay, back to my story... As my school year was ending I got a message through Facebook about a teaching position in MY hometown, the city I had always prayed to be able to give back to! My Facebook friend asked if I was looking for a job and I said 'YES'. I interviewed for the position, and low and behold, I got the job!

Now all I had to do was tell my current school 'goodbye'. It was indeed a hard thing to do because of all the relationships I built while I was there, but my leaving was necessary. I had finally come full circle and ended up right back where I had been trying to get to for about nine years.

Year one was the worst, best, challenging, blessed, and wonderful year ever! Oh, my God it was everything! Everything I thought it would be, hoped it would be, never expected it to be... some things I wished would never be again, and just down right draining.

I never knew how much I could change in a year. I remember one of my assignments during undergraduate year in college was to write our philosophy as an educator. I had that same philosophy for over twelve years.

No one told me that after my first year, my philosophy would change. I learned that nothing mattered other than reaching and changing the lives of my assignments (students). I realized who I was as a person. When I was in college, I was concerned with making sure that my assignments were always turned in a complete. Well, God told me to apply that same technique with my own students that were in my classroom. They were my assignments and I wanted them to be complete at the end of each school year.

So how was I going to do that? Though it may sound a little cliché, truth be told, it cannot be done except the Lord do it. The Holy Spirit gave (and continues to give) me wisdom to do what I do and reach those little souls grasping for knowledge. I mean, seriously, Who better to tell you what to do and what those kids needed than the Chief Architect Himself? Though the Holy Spirit was my guide, it had not always been easy. Those challenges were pushing me to purpose.

I feel like I am on a witness stand, about to raise my right hand and promise to tell the truth, the whole truth, and nothing but the truth so Help Me God! So here it is... the WHOLE truth!

I entered a classroom with a roll of my students' name, my pedagogy skills, or lack thereof I might add, a vow to my administrator and team, and a vow to God.

Once the door to the classroom closed behind me, I was on my own. It was time to put in practice everything I learned in theory. I, along with my grade level team, created a schedule that was the easy part. I learned very quickly that there were not enough hours in the day to complete the schedule.

How do you cope with feeling that you never got a chance to teach everything you wanted to teach? Between testing, extracurricular activities, lunch, and a few minutes for their mental break, it was time for the students to leave.

When you truly care about children and people, you tend to take things to heart. Because I was a new teacher I often dealt with the feeling of inadequacies. I remember I would walk next door to my colleague, now friend, sometimes and just see what she was doing to cope. I wanted to make sure that I was on task and doing good.

The Whole Truth & Nothing But the Truth, So Help Me Teachers!

God is so faithful that most of the time I found myself to be doing just fine. I would never forget one time I walked in and my friend was doing 'number talks'. Well, I had been out of college for quite some time before landing this job but none of my classes ever covered 'number talks'. I was blown away with this concept about student engagement that I wanted my students to experience it too. My friend graciously offered to come into my classroom to teach both me and my students about 'number talks'. I will never forget that because she really did not have to do that for me.

I guess I learned something about me too... whatever it took, my students wouldn't be left out. They were going to get everything they could possible get from me, even if it meant that I take professional development classes, workshops, or personal research. I never wanted the children assigned to me to not get what they needed for that year to be successful in school or just in life period.

So, you see, I don't take my assignments (students) lightly. I try to give my very best daily, all of me, withholding nothing from them. I often leave work with my voice gone. I haven't heard the sound of my voice (real voice) in months since school has been back in session. I try and leave everything I have each day. I realize it is necessary for where my students are going in life. I have had the pleasure of teaching and meeting some very bright children in my school district.

I learned that children, whether honor roll, gifted, or just average, all want the same thing from their teachers... and that is love and respect. Most importantly, I work to build a relationship with them before I begin teaching them anything. I let them know that they are safe to grow into their destiny.

I thank God for a forgiving spirit. I see how my students expect for me to hold things, but I make it my business to release them.

Even though they are eight or nine years old, somewhere along the line life taught them that you cannot recover from mistakes; but I teach against that. My philosophy is: today's a new day; what you did yesterday does not matter; you payed your due so the slate is wiped clean.

I can see their hearts changing. Plus, I want them to see the love of Christ through me. Every day they are greeted with a smile, and it does not matter if yesterday I had to frown to redirect back to destiny. Today is a new beginning because I realize I myself need grace every day too. So I also need to extend grace to my students. There are some challenges, do not get me wrong, but overall love is illustrated.

~  ~

The Whole Truth & Nothing But the Truth, So Help Me Teachers!

PART THREE: CLASS IN SESSION

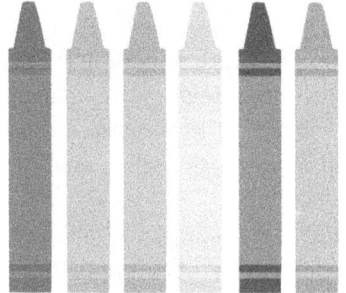

The Whole Truth & Nothing But the Truth, So Help Me Teachers!

Teresa Thomas

Wake Up America!

What exactly is the problem? Where do we start and who do we start with? How do we address the problems so we can collectively come up with viable solutions? When is the best time to start? Why should we attempt to challenge the status quo verses continuing on the path of least resistance? Who are the key people involved in facilitating these changes?

Why aren't all schools equipped and built equally with the same curriculum, financial budget for opportunities, processes and procedures for efficiency, quality staff and administration, and caliber of integrity?

Why are parents that want a quality education for their children forced to relocate into other municipalities to find the quality that they are looking for but still not welcomed?

As you can see I have questions and I definitely believe that we need answers. These questions sound simple but I realize the answer to these questions are complex in nature. What I really want people to understand is how we can make a difference and put more pressure on the political positions that are in place to help us make an impact.

It's time to stop passively accepting what is and challenge what we don't like. We have problems manifesting in the classroom because they are not addressed elsewhere, such as in the family, community, or even church. It's a spillover effect and it seems as if fingers are pointed in many different directions, but yet we still don't have solutions.

We have to stop for a moment and get involved in the working pieces that are going to help us function like a well-oiled machine. Yes, this is a big task but it is a task worth committing ourselves to.

The family is noted as your most important agent of socialization, then the school. My goal is to challenge these two spheres of influence in addition to the community to think about the answers to the questions listed above, and see how strategies can be developed to incorporate them in the primary function of the school.

We have to take a look at the roles that issues such as homelessness, single parent homes, two family homes with overworked parents, poverty, lack of finances and education from parents, and many more things play in building a strong foundation for education in 2017 going forward.

It's not that these areas have not been researched, but it's time to look at the research from a different perspective and start with accountable application.

When addressing a task of this caliber I believe there are key pieces of information that is needed in order to activate people in the direction of impact and engagement for the betterment of our children's education. This information will serve as a guide for parents, communities, community leaders, employees of our education system, educators, stakeholders and those aspiring to become more involved with improving the development of our children's education.

For some this will be the beginning of understanding, and for others it will be the key to help you understand the initial stages of how to create a strategy to address areas that need improvement in your local school systems. Some agree with the philosophy that ignorance is bliss but, today, I need you to understand that ignorance of this information will keep parents, stakeholders, communities, and educators in an inactivated state of living where little to no impact will ever be made and business will continue as usual.

It is time out to stop merely existing and start living on purpose when it comes to engaging with our children's education. It is not enough to support them in making good grades, being involved in school activities, and getting them prepared to pass standardized testing. That's a good start, but it's simply not enough to ignite change and initiate improvements in the areas where we see a need.

Think of this information as an awakening of your senses to the information you need to navigate as a parent, neighborhood partner, community leader, educator, or stakeholder in our children's development. Understand that no man or woman is an island by themselves. Regardless of how many children you have or if you don't have any at all, it is beneficial for you to understand that you are connected to a larger picture and you have an impact in that larger picture.

So here's the information you should consider:

1. *Get to know your State Department of Education.* Within the State Department of Education is a State Board of Education. The president of the Board is the governor of your state. Take some time to learn who the members of the board are, how many people sit on the board, what

districts they represent, how they are elected in, and when state board meetings are held. Find out who your state superintendent is as well as the duties coordinated with his or her role.

2. *Take the same approach as listed above about your State and learn about your city or county Board of Education.* Research information such as who are the members, how many people sit on the board? How are they elected and how long do they hold their positions? Who is the superintendent? When are the meetings? Where is the board of education?

3. *Understand that your property taxes matter!* Public schools are running off of the revenue that is collected from property taxes. This is not saying that this is the sole source of revenue but it is definitely a major contributor. How your schools are being funded is an essential piece of information that needs to be in your library of knowledge as a parent. If you pay property taxes, this thought alone should awaken your senses to a series of questions that have you wondering what can you do to help build a better education for your children.

4. *What role does or can your Mayor play in improving your child's education?* When you think of the responsibilities and duties of a Mayor, education may not be the first thing that comes to mind; however, while the Mayor may have limited authority in making direct decisions when it comes to our children's education, this role definitely has a seat at the table when it comes to partnering with those that have direct power. What we do in our communities' matter to our schools. In order to see change we must understand that the Mayor is a part of the village.

5. *Get to know your principal, vice principal, and staff.* Become partners with the vision and goals that they have in their role as principal. As a parent and educator, it is imperative that we embrace the understanding of

partnership with principals and their staff. Effective communication is key and parental involvement is a must. Taking on a combative relationship between principals and parents should never be the result that we see, but it happens. It is our responsibility as parents and educators to let our voices be heard and communicate with our principals. It is the responsibility of the principal and staff to welcome our parents and children into the vision and goals that are expected of them as principal. It is our responsibility together to hold each other accountable.

6. *Get to know your teachers. This is not as easy as you may think.* Being an educator and an involved parent, I definitely see two perspectives in how this engagement needs to take place. The key word again is *partnership*. Effective and clear communication is absolutely necessary in order for a great partnership to take place. As parents we should be clear about what our expectations are for our children, we should be aware of the classroom environment that our children are expected to perform in, and we should be onboard with the teacher in making efforts to enhance the learning process for not only our children but every child in the classroom. As teachers, it is our responsibility to always be transparent on what our goals and standards are in the classroom. Being realistic as parents and as teachers is going to help set the tone for how to engage and develop as partners in providing a great support system for our children as well as the progression of their academic goals.

7. *Parental Involvement is something that we cannot compromise in any form or fashion.* We owe it to our children, ourselves, and our society to get this right. We have to move beyond the basic outline that is expected of us and move into the deeper parts of how we need to function in order to make an impact on our children's education at large. We must go beyond good grades, passing standardized

testing, and having our kids involved in activities. These things are good, and I definitely recommend them, but the problem comes in when we stop there. The problem begins when there is more that is required from us but we can't give it because we are tied down by maintaining our own careers, providing for our households, and maintaining our entire families. Sometimes it feels like we don't have room for anything else but I encourage you to prioritize your priorities, never major on the minor, and to invest your time and energy in the areas that you excel in. Everybody has a unique set of skills and gifts that they can offer in the collective development of our children's education. Find that niche and build there. Don't get bogged down by the guilt of not being the parent that can be at the school all day, the parent that can decorate beautifully, or the parent that can be at meetings all the time. All these things are necessary and I am thankful that there are parents that are really good in these areas, but I encourage you to find out how you can serve. Identify what needs to be addressed in your child's school, and how you can partner with the principal and staff, and let your light shine. Get involved and stay engaged.

Taking these seven points into consideration will hopefully guide you into your next steps of understanding how you can go from just existing as a parent to becoming an active participant in the development of your child's education. The more you develop, the more you can help your child develop. It's not too late to engage yourself.

If we want to see a change in what's going on with some of the problems in the classroom, start here. I believe this approach can serve as a preventative measure to some of the issues that we as educators have faced and are facing in the classroom. It's a new day. Let's wake up to a new approach in how we move forward in the development of our children's education.

Final thought-provoking question is simply this: Are we going to stay complacent and complain, or are we going to get uncomfortable and make a difference? The choice is yours.

The Whole Truth & Nothing But the Truth, So Help Me Teachers!

Dalila Spratt

The Good, Bad & Ugly

Let me start by saying that I ABSOLUTELY love teaching!!! I have always wanted to be a teacher, since as early as 5-years-old. I can remember being in my bedroom as a child taking my night stand and pretending that it was a podium. I would teach my imaginary friends, Adie and John. Also, when I visited my great-grandmother I would pretend to teach the children on her block under her front porch.

There was a time, however, that I very much wanted to be a lawyer (I can be a bit argumentative). I had also wanted to be a news anchor. I even attended an orientation at Columbia College in Chicago for broadcast journalism. However, when I was told how I would be on call often, I figured that having a family may be difficult. So I went back to my FIRST love, TEACHING!

Now, I say this modestly: I really believe that teaching is my true gift from God! I say this because of the passion that I have for teaching and the joy it brings me. Now, don't get me wrong, I don't love every aspect of it. However, I really enjoy the interaction that I have with my students and, most of all, delivering a lesson.

When I'm up teaching, it's like a famous and most popular singer being on stage at a concert. You know, someone like Beyoncé or Michael Jackson. I am in my "natural" element doing my thing!

I must admit that I become very irritated when students, without warrant, interrupt me when I'm in my "mode". It is to the point that some students may think that I am mean. But really I am just passionate. Nevertheless, I am pretty tough because I desperately want my students to get from me what they need. Basically, I'm all smiles and hugs before and after class, but during instruction, I demand undivided attention. I take instruction very seriously.

I absolutely love delivering lessons, but one thing non-teachers may not realize is the planning that goes into a lesson can be simply overwhelming. To be honest, the thought of creating a lesson plan often gives me an anxiety attack, or the closest thing to one.

There is so much to consider when planning, I truly get flustered. I want to make my lessons engaging, make sure I appeal to all learning styles, make sure I reach all learners (because you can have several grade levels in one class), and possibly include technology.

Whatever happened to the good ole days when the teacher lectured and the students took notes (smile)? I know, I know... that's not the best approach, and definitely not my approach; but it used to work, at least it seemed to have worked for the generations that preceded mine. Now, it seems as though teachers need to wear clown suits with lights, bells, and whistles just to engage students.

For me, planning is definitely extremely stressful. When I begin to develop my lessons, I'm usually in my bed with my laptop or iPad. I surf several websites in search for ideas to incorporate with mine own to execute a great lesson. One day's lesson may take up to two hours to plan. I usually start fresh (at least I like to); I very rarely look at previous lesson plans. So, when the planning process begins, let's just say I am under duress.

With that being said, one thing that really saddens me about teaching is when kids are not interested in learning. I remember (about the second or third year in) feeling like I was fighting to pour knowledge into my students' heads. It seemed like education was some sort of disease that my students didn't want to catch.

At that time the media specialist at my school was retiring. In my frustration, I remember being outraged and going to my principal pleading to move me into that position when we returned from the Christmas vacation. I never realized how ridiculous it sounded considering that I didn't have the certification needed for that position, and I wouldn't be doing what I really loved to do.

You see, I have always loved learning and thought education was important, so I couldn't understand why so many students that I encountered had, what seemed like, the polar opposite perspective about education. I wanted so much for my students to love school as much as I did. In order to cope, I soon had to become a realist and understand that there are several variables that affect a student's approach to learning. In my evaluation, I realized that a major influence is social economics.

Ok, so let's venture off into my soap box issue – technology. I truly believe that the use of technology has had a GRAVE negative effect on student learning. Now I'm not delusional, I understand how our society has benefited from technology. But as it relates to our children, it has been overwhelmingly harmful. Many students spend countless hours using devices which are fast moving which I truly believe has contributed to an increase in attention deficit. I find that students have a really hard time paying attention during instruction, but it's pretty interesting that they can use a devise for extremely long periods of time, sometimes even forgetting to eat. As teachers, we are competing with technology.

Outside of delivering the lesson, I also enjoy the relationships I developed with my students. I ABSOLUTELY love all of them! This is not to say that some of them have not driven me completely crazy, but so have my own children (smile)!

Every year, there is usually a student or two that I developed a relationship with outside of school. Some years ago, I even allowed a student to travel with me to Chicago along with another teacher. Over the years, I had taken students out for a beauty salon or barber shop trip, to the circus, out to eat, shopping, and several other places. I attended church services, funerals, and family functions. For several of my former students, I have developed life-long relationships with and it feels good. Many of them I have the pleasure of keeping up with on Facebook. It warms my heart to see them finish school, get married, have children and engage in other endeavors.

As much as I love teaching, I have been gravely dismayed by the politics in education. Never in my wildest dreams would I have imagined that I would take witness to or be a part of the education "political" process, if you will.

One of the processes I am speaking to is the tenure law. This thing whereas a teacher can pretty much be non-renewed without even being told why. Basically, teachers are on a three year probation. You are assumed to be "safe" the first day of your fourth year. However, within the three year period, a teacher can just be let go without explanation sometimes.

Many times the decision for a teacher to be let go is made with bias and does not reflect any reason that deals with the educating of children. In many cases schools, school systems, and more importantly, the profession lose good teachers. For those who remain in education, the tenure law can be a real moral killer.

In the state in which I teach, tenure is only good for one school system. What this means is that if a teacher is let go within the three years from one school system and finds a job in another system, tenure starts over. A teacher can literally teach in five different school systems in five years-- so much for maintaining zeal.

Now let's talk about the T word... Testing. Everyone knows that near the end of the school year, filled with many lessons and activities, students are required to take a standardized test, assessing their knowledge of standards. There is a lot of pressure on teachers to make sure their students are up to par and, trust me, making that happen sometimes equates to being an amateur climber and taking on Mount Everest for your first climb.

The scrutiny that goes along with testing has even made some teachers take to cheating. I'm sure you've seen it in the news before.

TESTING may be the number one buzz word in education. When I was in school, I don't ever remember hearing the word until probably a week leading up to it. During that week, we had a special lunch. I remember having a hotdog, a bag of Jay's potato chips (I am a Chicago native), a pop (also known as a soda) and a Taffy apple. We preordered our lunch for the next week and administered the test. That's it.

Nowadays, there is so much focus on "the test" that law makers once said that a teacher's pay should be considered based on his or her test scores. Preposterous is what I was thinking. Ok, I get it. There should be some accountability, but that's taking things way too far to mess with a teacher's pay!

One of the aspects that make it difficult for teachers to raise test scores is the learning gaps that students may have. For example, a student who is in the seventh grade may read on the second grade level. So is one to assume that the teacher (at this point, the magician) is expected to get the child reading on grade level, provide quality work and be ready for a test on the seventh grade level by the end of the year? Now you follow me... But believe you me, as teachers, we try, even if it seems like it may be a long shot!

Last, but definitely not least, let's talk about teacher's salaries! It really amazes me how little teachers are paid for how much is expected of them. I remember a school professor defending our salaries by saying that teachers only work one hundred eighty two days compared to most people who work three hundred plus days a year. It made sense at first, it really did.

Then I started thinking about how many people have a job that actually ends when they leave for the day. When they say a teacher's job is never done, it's never done. I am always thinking about my students, planning for them, or purchasing something for them, not to mention the countless hours that goes into the sometimes daunting task of grading papers.

There have been times that I have been in the shower and had gotten the notion of a great lesson. And boy, you couldn't imagine how much of my personal money that I have spent towards my students. I often wonder if law makers take into consideration that a person's educational foundation is through a classroom teacher.

A teacher has taught pretty much every person in a high paying job and they don't see fit for teachers to have above average salaries. When I encounter people who are interested in becoming educators, I always tell them that they must go into the profession for the love of teaching and definitely not for the money, because our pay does not accommodate us for all that we do.

In closing, along with poor salaries, the overwhelming task of lesson planning, tenure law, testing, sometimes uninterested students, and classroom disruptions, I still ABSOLUTELY LOVE TEACHING!

I'll take the good, the bad, and the ugly. After 17 years in education, believe it or not, I have no desire to come out of the classroom. At this point, I could very easily see myself retiring as a teacher. I plan to carry on with my love, my craft.

The Whole Truth & Nothing But the Truth, So Help Me Teachers!

Katherine Lyons Bester

Lessons Along the Way

"And we'll understand it better by and by"... Growing up in the Baptist church, I heard these words sang so many times. Like most, I sang loud and proud, but I never quite understood what I was singing. Today, still sitting in that very same Baptist church, I sing with clarification, I understand.

In my mind, I somehow seemed to link my newfound understanding with my intent on finding the right career. I had a few snags along the way. However, there came a point in my life where it was clear to me that God had carefully orchestrated every step of my life, all to bring me to particular points and situations.

Even as a small child, I knew exactly what I wanted to do in life. For as long as I could remember, I wanted to be a Child Psychiatrist. Age seven was my first introduction to this career. I was sent to the school counselor. I was a quiet child but my teacher concluded that my lack of precociousness was simply because I, like many of my classmates, was terrified of the state-mandated test.

I do remember the overemphasis on the test. I thought "the test" was the most important thing ever! It seemed to be the thing all the teachers were concerned with at the time. In every class, there was constant talk of the test.

Years later as a teacher I'd find out why. It seemed the "test" bore an extreme amount of accountability. If children did well on the test, it was as though the teacher did well. If they didn't do well, this teacher was in the hot seat.

In hindsight, though, I'm not sure why my teacher reached the conclusion that the test frightened me. Tests never seemed to bother me. In my arrogance, I always assumed I'd pass them all. Whatever the reason my introduction to the school counselor was, it fueled my desire to help elementary-aged children.

Fast forward a few years, I got my first taste at helping children. I became an Elementary school teacher. Teaching was a likely career choice. It would not only give me the opportunity to help children, but it would also give me a place to show off some of the creativity many people believed I possessed. I loved it. For a while that is.

My first teaching assignment was second graders. I made my own bulletin boards, planned creative lessons and designed games that taught skills and concepts. For a few years, I was completely content. Then I began to want more.

I became very unhappy being a teacher. I didn't feel I was effective anymore. I was totally miserable because I was always focused on doing more. I began to feel as if I was doing more harm to the children I taught than anything.

My mind was consumed with doing everything, anything but teaching. And because of that, I was consumed with guilt. All I really wanted to do was help; and although I continued to teach and worked harder than ever, I decided to turn to the one thing I had always done well. I decided to become a student again.

I went back to school for an advanced degree to give me more career options. After completing my Masters in School Counseling, I landed my first job as an elementary school counselor. I was ecstatic! Finally, what I had planned to do with my life was somewhat coming to fruition. I was no psychiatrist, but the premise was the same. I would be a helper.

I've always had this overwhelming desire to help anyone who needed it. There were many causes that became dear to my heart, most evolved around the neglecting or abuse of children.

As most counselors, I also tried hard to help children develop better character. There were always lessons on anger management techniques, self love, respect, friendship and kindness. However, this job also came with the awesome responsibility of problem solving. A school counselor in an elementary school is looked upon as the person who helps to solve problems that teachers might not otherwise have time to. I absolutely loved this job so I always did my best. The children seemed to trust me, and I had finally found my niché.

In this position there were many causes that I wanted to champion. Of all the causes I tackled as a school counselor, there always seemed to be one particular cause that always seemed to resonate with me. It was a cause that rarely directly affected children. This cause was breast cancer.

From the moment I became a counselor, I worked tirelessly every year in October during Breast Cancer Awareness Month to educate people about breast cancer and to raise money to contribute to the cure. I never understood why, I just did. On May 16, 2015, my understanding became clearer.

As I was ending another great year of learning to be the best counselor I could, I was faced with the biggest scare of my life. I was diagnosed with breast cancer. Now for anyone this was a grim diagnosis, but for me, a lifetime hypochondriac, it was too much to bear.

You see, I'd always been overly concerned about my health. Even as a child, a simple headache in my mind was just the making of an aneurism, a stomach ache was an ulcer, and of course, any pain was thought to be the dreaded big "C", cancer! I was constantly complaining about something hurting, and although I had experienced firsthand every simple childhood illness there was, in my mind they were all dreadful diseases. Somewhere early on in life, I became preoccupied with dying.

Looking back, I attribute that to losing a lot of family members early in life. Coming from a very large family (twenty six uncles and aunts), it seemed to me that someone was always dying. What was really so bad was my preoccupation sometimes hindered me from living. I often chose to stay in rather than go out. I chose to sit rather than dance and often positioned myself around those that cried, rather than those that laughed. What resulted was a deep feeling of being unfulfilled. I was too scared to die, but just as scared to live.

The breast cancer diagnosis consumed me and my family. Although no day would have been ideal, cancer showed up at an inopportune time. May 16, 2015 was the very last day of school. It was also a day my family will never forget. My 24-year-old cousin Jade, two weeks prior had given birth to her third child and first son. There were no complications with the birth but shortly afterwards she developed pneumonia. The pneumonia was so severe it caused serious damage to her lungs. On that same day of my diagnosis, the family was called to the hospital. We were told that Jade would not live to see the morning.

As my mother and I rushed to the hospital, I got a call from my doctor. That call would change my life as I knew it. The doctor said that the biopsy I had taken two weeks earlier had come back positive for breast cancer. He said he needed me to come in to see him immediately. My concern for my cousin soon turned to complete devastation and fear. Selfishly, I could only think of myself. I was afraid for my life.

At the very same time, somewhere inside of me, I was afraid for Jade's life also. During the call, I'm sure the doctor said many things. To this day, I have no idea what he said. Everything went silent. I remember only thinking, "I can't do this! I have a child to raise! I can not die!" I remember hanging up the phone and crying uncontrollably. My mother who was driving, remained calm. She said simply, "Whatever we have to do, we will do it. You will be fine." I'm not sure how I remember that, but as time went on, one of the few things that was always clear on this journey where a lot was hazy, were the words of my mother.

After arriving at the hospital, my emotions completely took control of my body. I went to a very dark place. The devil had completely robbed me of my faith. In my mind, I was going to die. Prior history had made the word cancer to me synonymous with death. Four years earlier this idea was rooted and planted in my mind. In one month, my father who is one of ten children lost three of his siblings. Two out of three died of cancer. That was one of the most emotionally draining times in my life. I cried openly for weeks, and the loss added to my unhealthy fears.

A few months prior to my initial diagnosis, I experienced quite a few symptoms. I had extreme itching on both my breasts, a dull achy pain in the center of my breasts, and one breast grew much larger than the other. Four biopsies and several disagreements between the radiologists and my doctor later, a diagnosis came.

The day of the diagnosis was draining for my family. They were torn in two dark directions. My cousin Jade was critically ill and I had been given a dire diagnosis.

I was inconsolable. All of my family members tried to console me, including three uncles who had been diagnosed also with cancer. Two of the three were diagnosed in early stages and were doing well. The other had battled and beaten cancer five times, but he was growing weary. His words to me were frightening. He painted a very dark picture of what I should expect. Thankfully, God stepped in. Although my uncle continued to talk to me, there came a point when I could no longer hear him. I only remember the words of my mother. She looked sternly at me and said, "We will beat this! I don't care if houses are gone, cars...whatever! You're not going anywhere! Between God, my in-laws, and us, we got this!"

Thinking back I realized that my mother's tone, determination and unconditional love got me through that day. Her words gave me hope that somehow I was going to get through this nightmare. Guilt crowded my heart. I desperately wanted to see my cousin Jade. I knew however, if I saw her in the state described to us by doctors, I would be consumed with sadness for her and fear for myself. I never made it to my cousin's hospital room that night.

Thankfully, the doctors were wrong. Jade pulled through that day, and by God's grace and mercy, she's alive and healthy today. The very next day my parents, husband and I went to see the Oncologist. He walked in with a nurse practitioner and an intern. They all walked in smiling with extended arms ready for hugs. The doctor was a very jolly looking Caucasian man. He had a big bright smile and rosy cheeks. He came in with a notepad and a plan.

Regardless of his intentions, I had only one question, "How are we going to save my life?" The doctor embraced me as if he was reading my mind, then said, "You're gonna be okay. I had cancer myself four years ago, I am fine."

He turned to all of my family members and said, "We have several routes we can take for treatment. You have what's called non-invasive breast cancer. There is a mass that is centralized in your left breast. We can do a lumpectomy to remove it, followed by chemotherapy and radiation, or we can treat this radically which is what I suggest. Now that means for six months we give you the strongest chemo we have, Adriamycin and Cytoxan, a bilateral mysectomy and thirty rounds of radiation."

My family all spoke in unison, "Let's do that!" I agreed.

The doctor looked at me and then said, "You're young, you can do this. Don't worry!" He then turned to my family and began to explain to them that this was a journey that would be hard for all of us. He explained that at times it would be harder for them than it would be for me because they would experience helplessness. He also said that they will want to help me but all they really could do for me was to pray and offer support.

The doctor was very pleasant, so much so that he could easily moonlight as Santa Claus. With his rosy cheeks, white hairy beard and kind demeanor, he was exactly what I needed. Despite the doctor's bedside manner, I began to cry. Just the mention of the treatment plan was frightening, and it did indeed sound like a journey. My family insisted that I would be okay. What was terrifying though was their words said it will be ok, but the look on their faces showed incredible fear.

I left the hospital that day with the daunting task of telling my children and the rest of my family about the diagnosis. I thought of my daughters, how would they react to the news. I thought about my job, and wondered what would my principal say. How was I supposed to leave it for fifteen months, be able to help my husband with the household bills and still keep my job? I thought about my church and my pastor. I needed them to intercede, plead with God on my behalf. I thought about my family and friends. I knew they'd all be as devastated as I was when they heard the words from my mouth...I have cancer.

To my surprise, my children took it very well. They were very supportive and not fearful at all. My girls who were ages 13 and 19 at the time were my rocks. Although, initially I tried to shield my 13-year-old by saying I had a breast 'infection'. She figured out the truth, came to me and said, "I know you have cancer, but you're going to be OK."

That day my girls got together with a box of envelopes, and wrote a supportive and biblical letter for every situation they thought would arise on my journey. There was one that read, "After you finish chemotherapy"; another one that read, "Open when you're afraid"; and even one that said, "Open when you're cancer free!" along with many others. I was so honored and so proud. These two girls had learned what cancer was making me forget: with Christ all things are possible.

I got the same support from family members. There were visits, calls and prayers. They all wanted to help any way they could. I even got great support from work. My friend Linda stood by my side constantly, and my principal and former principal called to check on me frequently.

My husband took the news very hard. A few days later after watching him cry continuously, I awoke to find him on the side of the bed. He was crying yet again. I looked at him and asked, "How am I supposed to believe that I'm not going to die, if you do? You have me feeling as if I'm doomed." He looked up at me and agreed. From that point on, he was as supportive as he knew how to be.

The most shocking thing about this journey was the reactions of my "friends". My circle had always been small, so I didn't have many to tell about my diagnosis. There were a few tried and true friends who remained supportive throughout my entire journey.

As you would expect, from the beginning all of my "friends" had very similar responses as my family. They were sorry and prayerful. Needless to say that didn't last very long. I had a few friends, including the person I thought was my best friend, who treated this cancer diagnosis as as if the doctor had told me I had a cold. They were simply uncaring and unconcerned.

I even remember having a conversation with my supposedly best friend. At the time I had been in treatment about nine months. I asked her why she never called or came by to visit. She went on to tell me that she was busy and had her own issues in life (the same issues she'd had since meeting her 20 years prior). Needless to say, I realized two things really quick: One, this person, along with a few others who reacted similarly, were and never had been my friend; and two, God was yet again mapping out my journey. He was removing negative people from my life. Although, it was one of the most painful things on this journey, I listened to God's voice, and let them walk away.

Thankfully, God had a plan. My circle became larger. Acquaintances I had all my life showed themselves to be true and genuine friends. I was constantly getting flowers, phone calls, gift cards, books and texts. The outpouring of support was amazing.

The next fifteen months were the most difficult and faith-filled days of my life. Emotionally, I was all over the place. I went from, today I'm going to live to today I'm going to die. This was made exceptionally harder through the loss of my uncle who had beaten cancer five times before. His death tainted me! I was convinced that if he had to fight five times and still lost the battle, then there was no hope for me. I was so consumed with his death, I never went to the funeral. To this day, I regret that. I loved my uncle. I miss him.

Although, I spoke often to God before this diagnosis, during this turbulent time, I often heard Him speak to me. He had become my closest friend. He literally carried me through this journey. I'll never forget during one of my darkest days before treatment, I was in the middle of yet another crying spell, I heard the voice of my favorite uncle who had died four years earlier. He said as clear as if he was sitting near me, " You will not die of cancer. Cancer will not kill you!" With those words, I mustered up the courage to begin treatments. Chemotherapy was first.

I had to have six months of poison pumped into my body to kill the cancer cells. My mother took me to every visit. I was placed in a room with 10-12 other patients who were also undergoing chemotherapy. We sat in big comfy recliners as the nurses on duty ran the chemotherapy intravenously. I did pretty well with chemotherapy. There were many side effects I watched others go through. I was blessed only to experience nausea and extreme fatigue. I prayed constantly. I meditated and even recited scriptures that were given to me by good friends. I was armed for battle. I was armed with the Word of God to beat cancer.

After my very first chemo treatment, I began to lose my hair. I literally reached up to touch my hair and it began falling in clumps in my hand. I called my new friend and neighbor Tiffany, who was a beautician. I went to her house and amidst tears and prayer, Tiffany shaved my head. It was very symbolic. The act created a bond with her that will never be broken. It was really the first visual sign that I had cancer.

My husband asked me to call the wife of one of his friends. He heard that she too had breast cancer. I contacted her. To my surprise we were on very similar roads on our journey. She and I became friends and a huge support for each other. We talked constantly, shared our paths and prayed together.

Support also came in another surprising package. My husband's ex-wife was extremely supportive. She and I had always been cordial, but my illness made us friends. She constantly called and checked on me, bought gifts and even introduced me to a friend who was going through her own journey. Her friend was a previvor. She had breast cancer in her family so she opted to have a bilateral mastectomy to prevent the risk of later in life getting cancer. Turns out the three of us walked the similar paths for months. Having two people to talk to who were feeling exactly the same thing you were at the exact same time was a God send.

We all had surgery within weeks of the other. Around this time, I received the most shocking news ever. On a routine doctor's visit I found out that I had stage three cancer. I was floored. For the past two years, I had been getting mammograms every six months. They were all negative. Again, the devil raised his ugly head. Again, I became terrified for my life. But just as soon as fear took over, faith stepped in. As if seeing a movie of my life, I began to see how God had carried me through each step. From detection to diagnosis, to a loss of so-called friends and frightening treatments. God carried me.

The next step in my treatment was the most difficult. I had a bilateral mastectomy with reconstruction. It was a surgery that lasted 9 1/2 hours. I remember thinking about my family and how scared they would be for 9 1/2 hours. Ironically enough, although I had been fearful in the days leading to the surgery, the day of, I was fine. Somehow I got this amazing peace that only God could give. I knew going into surgery that God would again carry me through. I remember leaving my family and heading to the operating room. I knew I had everything I needed and I would be just fine. I was, of course, right.

However, this surgery was yet another difficult time in my life. It was a hard recovery but it was made much easier on December 1st when the doctor came in and informed me that I was cancer free! They had gotten all of the cancer in surgery. I've had many great days in my life, the birth of my children, my wedding, graduations, but this day was right up there with them all! I felt I had been given back my life. Because of the great news, my efforts in physical therapy and my willingness to go home, I was slated to be discharged a few days later.

The Whole Truth & Nothing But the Truth, So Help Me Teachers!

On the day of my discharge, my surgeon who had come in to approve the discharge noticed something alarming. My heart rate was beating 40-50 times faster than normal. This had been going on for days, but no one seem alerted. The surgeon immediately ordered a cat scan. Needless to say, that day a blood clot was found in each of my lungs. Again the power of Jesus Christ saved me because had this gone undiscovered, I could have died.

I spent a few days in the hospital on blood thinners. I was just thankful that God was continuously showing me signs that He was the leader on this journey. This all happened during my favorite time of year, the holidays. When I finally got to go home, I chose to recover by staying with my mother (a nurse) until I was better. This meant my husband and daughter would stay there as well. We stayed for one month. I couldn't walk for the first few days, I was in extreme pain and I could not take care of any of my hygienic needs. I could not move my arms, and I had six breast pumps (filled with blood and tissue) hanging from my breasts and back. I even had to sleep sitting up in a recliner. My mother attended to all of my needs.

She also made sure my state of mind was good. She constantly talked to me, tried to entertain me and made sure that no one brought any stress my way. My entire family was focused on my recovery. My brother and sister bought me gifts and made me laugh to keep my spirits high. My father constantly reminded me of God's power, and my husband and children remained by my side through everything. On the day before Christmas, I went home to my house.

Although I wasn't quite well, my mother agreed to allow me to be at home for Christmas. I was stunned to find my husband, and two brother-in-laws cleaning and cooking upon my return. They invited over the neighbors, who had become some of my closest friends. We had a ball. I was yet again overwhelmed by the outpouring of support. Most importantly for the first time in a year, I had fun! I was thrilled to be home. Everyone there took really good care of me.

Next on the treatment list was radiation. I had thirty treatments to do. I found the first 25 treatments to be extremely easy, I simply laid down on a table and lights passed over me for about five minutes. Then I drove myself home. It was a breeze, up until treatment 26, the radiation began to burn. It burned my reconstructed breasts, and my neck so badly they blistered. Although the doctor provided creams for relief, it was no fun at all.

But finally for a while, hospital treatments would stop. During this time, I experienced yet another blow. My father-in-law whom I loved dearly passed alway suddenly. It took a huge toll on my family, especially my husband. Although I managed to go to the funeral, this was a real tough time. Mentally and emotionally, I was a mess! I had two surgeries pending, a plethora of daily meds and an entirely new body, somehow I had to rest and recover.

To sum it all up: Cancer was the worst thing that ever happened to me personally, but there were so many blessings that God gave me to bring me through it! I can never repay my doctors! They were and still are awesome!

Cancer helped my marriage. My husband was able to again see my worth after the prospect of losing me, and I could clearly see his. We have never been closer.

My daughters, who were already strong, now know that they can do all things through Christ. They knew that if a hypochondriac like me could make this journey and win, they could do anything!

The Whole Truth & Nothing But the Truth, So Help Me Teachers!

My Principal and my coworkers are loving, patient and supportive; my church family keeps me in prayer; my mother is my constant nurse and biggest fighter; my father, my siblings and my family never let me forget what God has done for us; my friends that God gave me through this illness are the best I've ever had! They sense all fear, pray for my peace of mind and are determined to help me stay cancer free and enjoy life!

I am so thankful to God! He healed me one December day! Most of all, He healed my heart and mind as well. I have no ill-will towards anyone anymore! I forgive everything, my discernment is keen and I'm clear about who loves me! I have the best support system ever, but on this journey no one loved me like Jesus Christ! I still have a ways to travel, but I know I have a traveling partner who will never leave me alone!

The Whole Truth & Nothing But the Truth, So Help Me Teachers!

Carole Cramer-Banks

A Moment of Transparency

Dear Readers is how I started my musing that I'd written to my readers on my blog, *Special 2 Me*, for the last couple of years. Even though I don't know any of my readers in real life, it has always been my hope that I would be able to affect their lives with every story that I write.

I'd like to do the same for you, *Dear Readers*. Take what you need from my experience as you read my story to help you in your life. Let's begin!

Dear Readers...I'm unsure of which way to proceed. When I decided to write for this book, I was going to write something cloying and totally unrealistic. I was going to gloss over just how difficult teaching can be. However, I didn't want to be 'that teacher'! I didn't want to be that person who would potentially be the one who would dissuade someone from following their dream of becoming a teacher. You know that person who's a Negative Nelly.

Over the past couple of years, I'd hit rock bottom over and over again, just to pull myself up by my bootstrap. When I thought I couldn't possibly go back to work in that classroom and deal with another teenage attitude, I did!

This thing called teaching is a helluva rollercoaster ride. I've been up and down more than the Twisted Colossus at Magic Mountain amusement park.

Right now, I'm currently on a downward spiral. I thought I'd always want to teach, but now, that's not the case. I'd like to start from the beginning, but I honestly don't know where the beginning is. I mean, as I write this, I'm sitting in my living room at 11 o'clock at night, doing some 'oh, so important internet surfing!'

What should I be doing? I should be writing my submission for this book that I felt was my destiny to be a part of. I should be getting ready for tomorrow's lessons, but I simply cannot muster up the courage to do that because I'm not sure if I want to continue in my chosen vocation of teaching.

It's not all that I thought it would be. Of course, nothing ever is, is it? That's what I've been telling myself because I've been too afraid to try; too afraid to be the best version of myself I can be. I stopped challenging myself. I let everything get me down.

When a student gave me attitude, I took it personally. When one of my colleagues had something to say about a Special Education student, I took it personally! How could I not? I mean, I am the Special Education Teacher extraordinaire, aren't I?! Who would dare to speak a harsh word against my students?! Well, there were some who did. They even had the nerve to think they could speak badly about them in my presence. The nerve, right?!

Coddler Extraordinaire & No Child Left Behind!

Well, in order to combat those who would unfairly prejudiced my students simply because of something that happened to the wiring of their brain before they were born, I went out of my way to ensure that my students were not affected by the negativity. I wanted to make sure that they were taken care of; that they were given every single accommodation written into their Individualized Education Program (I.E.P.). In fact, I went overboard. I coddled them way too much to ensure that not one of them were left behind.

Ever since the first year though, I'd been questioning whether or not I made the right decision to teach. Everyone thought I was crazy when I accepted the Elementary Special Day Class (SDC) teaching position right next to the Nickerson Gardens housing projects. I knew I was in for a treat (said sarcastically!).

The first day was as expected. The second, third, fourth, fifth, sixth... days were so hard, complicated by the fact that I was working full-time, in school full-time, and a mother to four children, ages ranging from 5-17. I know I am not the first and I know that I will not be the last to do that; many have gone through this.

Where I went wrong is when I tried to be too strong and be superwoman. After losing my voice, contracting the flu twice within a 6-week period, and having walking pneumonia all before Christmas break, I quickly learned that I was not SUPERWOMAN! We all need a support system.

That moment was the time when I learned a very important lesson in my life: No man is an island! I had my husband, my mother, six sisters, a couple of very good sister-friends, and an extra-large extended family; so there was no need to do it by myself. I am really not sure why I tried to do it by myself in the first place now that I think about it. But after recuperating during Christmas break, I resolved to take advantage of and use my support system.

I'd been in the Education field for 15 years. The first 5 1/2 years, I was a Special Education Assistant. I transitioned to teaching in 2007, after graduating from Azusa Pacific University (APU) in Azusa, California, with a Bachelors in Human Development.

Immediately after graduating with my Bachelors, I entered the Masters in Education Specialist Credential Program at Loyola Marymount University (LMU) in Westchester, California. My first major teaching heartbreak was during my time at LMU.

At the time, LMU's Teaching Program catered to Teach for America (TFA) students. When teachers in the TFA program ran into any type of problem, big or small, with their placement, the powers that be jumped into action and helped them change their placement or intervened in some way.

Since I was not in TFA, I was not considered part of the upper echelon of the teachers in the School of Education. Any thoughts I had about being afforded the same consideration was dashed once I ran into trouble with an emotionally unstabled and irate parent who sought to do me harm. Since I was not part of TFA, I was ignored by the School of Education and left to fend for myself. I took a leave of absence due to stress for about two months, during which time I was railroaded by the principal and eventually blacklisted from the school district.

Because of all that I experienced, I changed my way of thinking about the term "learning disabilities". I wish I thought this way when I first started teaching my first band of misfits. I kinda' feel bad for all the years that I'd been telling students that they have disabilities. It's so ironic that I'd come to this conclusion because I always felt that having students accept that they had a disability was what led to them to becoming a better version of themselves.

There's nothing I can do about the past though. It's like that old saying, "if I had known then what I know now..." However, moving forward, I'm not going to tell my students that they have learning disabilities; I'm telling them that they have learning differences. Every year, in the Resource Lab, I teach the students "how" they're smart with the Multiple Intelligence Survey. I then give them several other surveys and questionnaires.

My first group of students is graduating in June. These were the ones I coddled from the beginning. Save one, they are self-sufficient students who advocate for themselves. They know how they learn.

No Quick and Dirty Answer

Here's the thing... there is no quick and dirty answer. I would like to say that I have the answer, that I woke up the day after I wrote this and edited it to reflect my changed mindset; but I have not. I am still on the fence about whether or not to leave teaching. In fact, I'm not even going into work tomorrow. I'm taking a mental health day. If you need it, I suggest you do the same!

The Whole Truth & Nothing But the Truth, So Help Me Teachers!

Delores "Magnolia" Walker

A Simple Reminder

September 1990-Rural Classroom USA

The fired-up rookie looked around at the controlled chaos in the classroom. Paper scraps, crayons and scissors litter the polished wooden floor of the near century old school building. The class had completed a chapter on the water cycle the day before. According to the Quality Core Curriculum (QCC) the teacher had covered the required information.

However, being young and incredibly motivated she was taking their learning to the next level. She understood the importance of auditory, visual and tactile learning being integrated into the lesson plan. She hummed softly to herself as she walked through the slippery landmine of engaged learners. Blonde straight-haired heads and dark curly (kinky) haired heads touched as leaned close to whisper. (Lest some other group hear and steal their idea).

Just two short decades' earlier, light-skinned hands would not be holding cotton balls for darker-skinned hands to glue down. Integration had come slowly and painfully to this small town. But, it was proving very valuable for its future. Already, shared ideas not just in the classroom, but in the community was proving fruitful.

Ashleigh McDougald looked down at her watch, "So class lets clean our area and pack up." There were a few murmurs of protests from the very dedicated ones. However, they quickly followed directions. Ashleigh completed a quick walk through and pointed out the stray piece of paper or forgotten crayon.

Without needing a reminder, the class helpers quickly retrieved the brooms and dustpans. They made quick work of the remaining scraps of paper and returned to their seats.

Just then the first dismissal bell sounded. Instead of changing from controlled to uncontrolled chaos, as it had in early days, the students simply paused and looked to their teacher for her signal. Without raising her voice she asked, "Does everyone have their homework copied into your agenda?" She made it a point to make eye contact with each of her students. As expected, Marshall became very focused on zipping his book bag.

Ashleigh walked quickly to his side. "Hey let me initial yours okay? I promised Mom, that I would check behind you. We don't want a repeat of last week do we?"

Ashleigh had called Marshall's mom, a single mom, because his grades were dropping and his homework was incomplete. They had discovered that Marshall was only copying half of his assignments. It was impossible to get upset with him when they realized that he wanted to rake yards and help his mother. He thought that if he brought in extra money, she wouldn't have to leave before the school bus and he wouldn't have to listen to his older sister.

Ashleigh noticed that Math problems #1-10, had somehow become #1-3. She made the correction, initialed and handed it back to him as the second bell rang. Still, the class waited patiently.

Ashleigh called out, "Tuesday's row." Quickly and quietly that row lined up the door, followed by each of the remaining days and ending with Monday. She signaled for them to walk out in a single filed line, in an orderly fashion.

Looking around she noticed that Scott had left his sharpened pencil on his desk. This would be a problem, seeing that few children had extra writing utensils at home. She picked up his pencil and caught him in the hallway. She slipped the pencil into his book bag and escorted her class outside to the parking lot to load the buses.

Ashleigh was not assigned a specific bus to monitor, instead she was one of the teachers assigned to watch and make sure no students lingered inside the building or darted out the backdoor. After checking the restrooms, both boys and girls, she went back outside the building. She heard a couple of students yelling her name out of the window. She managed to both respond and admonish them for yelling simultaneously.

As soon as the last bus was safely on its way, she headed back to her classroom. She had fifteen minutes before the faculty meeting started. She briefly debated on whether she needed to start grading those two sets of papers or take a much needed restroom break. Her bladder strongly asserted itself and won the argument. She darted to the restroom after grabbing a notepad and some loose change from her desk. She perused the snack machines before settling on a Pepsi and a pack of peanut butter cookies.

Ashleigh was the first one in the cafeteria. After brushing off some forgotten crumbs, she staked out a seat nearest to the exit. She wished she had returned to her classroom and grabbed those papers. She could have used the old "I'm taking notes, but secretly grading papers" technique. She had managed to perfect this technique in no time at all.

The principal entered and, as if on cue, the rest of the faculty followed. After clearing his list of normal teacher meeting mentionables, the principal began listing important upcoming dates.

Ashleigh dutifully copied the information into her notebook. As he completed his list, her mind shifted off. She was just imagining her one-on-one interview with Denzel Washington when she realized there was an eerie silence. She quickly snapped back to attention.

Her co-workers were looking at her expectantly. She looked across the table at her grade level representative who mouthed the words "My Teacher is Tops". Ashleigh stood nervously and the room burst into applause. Apparently one of her students had written into the local news station and nominated her for this honor.

A little earlier in the week Ashleigh had questioned her decision to be a teacher. An uncomfortable parent/teacher meeting, a lesson plan that went south, and chapter test grades that tanked had shaken her belief in herself.

But this award was affirmation. Maybe she would stick around another ten or twenty years. Time would tell.

The Whole Truth & Nothing But the Truth, So Help Me Teachers!

Acknowledgments

From the Desk of the Compiler, Vicki Kirk May

To my husband, my greatest support, thank you for loving me through every word, sentence, and paragraph. Stan, those nights you cooked dinner and fixed your lunch means more than you know.

Jessica (daughter): There aren't many mothers who are lucky enough to have a daughter like mine. Thank you Jessica for always reminding me that I am an author, and authors write.

Matt (son): You have given me my "why", and whenever I wanted to quit, it was Nacaria and Naya who kept me going.

Rene, Eric, and Kevin (siblings): By watching you all be amazing makes me believe that I can be amazing as well. I truly appreciate your support throughout this entire process.

Eric (brother): I shared my vision with you once and that was all it took. You created the perfect book cover and I love you for bringing it to life. My wish is that you make thousands and thousands more visions become a reality.

To every educator who wakes up intentionally and in purpose daily in order to change the world one day at a time, I salute.

The Whole Truth & Nothing But the Truth, So Help Me Teachers!

About the Compiler

VICKI KIRK MAY

Vicki Kirk May is a 20-year-veteran educator in the State of Alabama. Vicki received a degree in Elementary Education with honors. With all that she has accomplished, her biggest accomplishment is her family.

Being a wife, mother, daughter, sister, grandmother, and ordained minister of the Gospel is true success to Vicki. She is driven by her passion and purpose to change the lives of children and educators. Known as the Passion Accelerator, Vicki believes that we all were endowed with gifts and passions to change the world, and that those gifts and passions should not be limited by the four walls of your classrooms, offices, or minds but unleashed to effectuate change in the world and lead you to your abundance.

As a result of Vicki's beliefs and becoming so frustrated being in a state of complacency, she founded Passion Without Walls LLC, a business designed to support educators who are ready to take their passion beyond the classroom and church through entrepreneurship. The Passion Accelerator is a personal development, leadership and team-building strategist who goes into schools, churches and businesses to shape, form, and create strong leaders and effective teams. Understanding that low teacher/leader morale is real and it does exist, Vicki supports educators and ministry leaders through personal development, leadership and team-building training.

Vicki specializes in helping educators and ministry leaders identify and gain clarity on their passion and monetize it. As a minister of the gospel, she finds fulfillment in helping others find purpose through the word of God and live the abundant Life that is their birthright.

You can connect with Vicki via the following:

 Vicki Kirk May

 @vickikirkmay

 vkirkmay_

 passionwithoutwalls@gmail.com

~ 🍎 **THE END** 🍎 ~

www.ingramcontent.com/pod-product-compliance
Lightning Source LLC
Chambersburg PA
CBHW070201100426
42743CB00013B/3001